SILENT SPACES

The Last of the Great Aisled Barns

SILENT SPACES

The Last of the Great Aisled Barns

MALCOLM KIRK

A BULFINCH PRESS BOOK

LITTLE, BROWN AND COMPANY   Boston • New York • Toronto • London

For Bryce

After Isis had discovered the fruit of both wheat and barley
which grew wild over the land . . .
and Osiris had also devised the cultivation of these fruits,
all men were glad to change their food
. . . because of the pleasing nature of the newly discovered grains . . .
Even yet at harvest time the people make a dedication
of the first heads of grain to be cut,
and standing beside the sheaf beat themselves and call upon Isis,
by this act rendering honor to the goddess
for the fruits which she discovered,
at the season when she first did this.

Diodorus of Sicily, first century B.C.

First Edition

ISBN 0-8212-2093-4
Library of Congress Catalog Card Number 94-3863

Bulfinch Press is an imprint and trademark of Little, Brown and Company (Inc.)
Published simultaneously in Canada by Little, Brown & Company (Canada) Limited

Frontispiece: The barn of the Manoir du Mont-St.-Michel
at Bretteville-sur-Odon in Calvados, Normandy.

PRINTED IN ITALY

CONTENTS

ACKNOWLEDGMENTS

Without the generous assistance of the people and institutions listed below, this book might never have reached fruition. By acknowledging their contribution, however, I do not mean to convey the impression they necessarily endorse my own views. The majority of these individuals have distinguished academic credentials. I hope they will forgive me, therefore, for omitting their full titles, out of respect for others who have none but who have made notable contributions in their own right.

In Belgium: Marc Laenen.

In Denmark: Hans Engqvist and Frode Kirk.

In France: Bernadette Barrière, Bernard Baton, Bibliothèque et Archives du Patrimoine (Paris), Centre de Documentation de L'Inventaire (Paris), Centre des Recherches sur les Monuments Historiques (Paris), André Guilbert, Terryl Kinder, Christian Lassure, Claire and Patrick Lefebvre, Elizabeth Lescroart-Cazenave, Bruno Malinverno, Alain Marais, Jean Marie Perouse de Montclos, Marcel and Lionel Plasmans, Léon Pressouyre, Nicolas Sainte-Beuve, François Verdier, and Jacques Vico.

In Germany: Claus Ahrens, Konrad Bedal, Ralf Busch, Hermann Claussen, Heinz Ellenberg, Herman Hinz, Fred Kaspar, Joachim Kleinmanns, Dietrich Maschmeyer, Cornelia Meier, and the Westfälisches Baupflegeamt.

In the Netherlands: Herman Hagens, H. A. Heidinga, Carlo Huijts, Ellen van Olst, Nico Roymans, Frans Theuws, and H. T. Waterbolk.

In Switzerland: Benno Furrer and Max Gschwend.

In Tunisia: Ben Younes-Habib and the Musée du Bardo.

In the United Kingdom: Philip Aitkens, Jim Alexander, the British Library, Gretel Boswijk, Freddie and Mary Charles, Glyn Coppack, R. Dockeray, Nigel Harvey, Barbara Hutton, English Heritage, Cecil Hewett, Edward Impey, Adrian James, Peter Kidson, John Lacey, David and Barbara Martin, John McCann, Gwyn Meirion-Jones, Bernard Nurse, Michael Peach, The National Trust, Winifred Phillips, Oliver Rackham, Peter Reynolds, Geoffrey Rickman, Peter Ryder, John Sell, W. John Smith, Peter Smith, The Society of Antiquaries, M. S. Spurr, Neil Stratford, Jane Wade, John Weller, and K. D. White.

In the United States: Margaret Alexander, the Avery Library, Columbia University, New York, James Bartsch, Rainer Berger, Constance Berman, Roderic Blackburn, Ben Brungraber, Joseph Campbell, David Cohen, Michael Davis, Giles Constable, Lynn Courtenay, Peter Fergusson, Charles Gehring, Bernadette Glasse, Frank Hole, The Illinois Research and Reference Center, Mary Littauer, Robert Loomis, Claire Lyons, the Institute of Fine Arts, New York, the New York Public Library, Paul and Nora Petrescu, the Pierpont Morgan Library, New York, Lorna Price, Lawrence Richardson, Berta Rudofsky, David Sauer, Glen Schwartz, Brent Sverdloff, Peter Wacker, Gene Waddell, Walter Widrig, and Harold Zoch.

I am profoundly grateful to the Getty Center for the History of Art and the Humanities, Walter and Alberta Horn, John T. and Heather Smith, and Haio and Gundel Zimmermann, who have been particularly helpful and hospitable.

My thanks also to Karen Dane, Peggy Freudenthal, Brian Hotchkiss, and Betty Power for their guidance as editors and to Michael Levins, who made the fine black-and-white prints.

Last but not least, credit for assembling the material for this book must go to my gracious partner and friend, Bryce Birdsall. She also happens to be my wife.

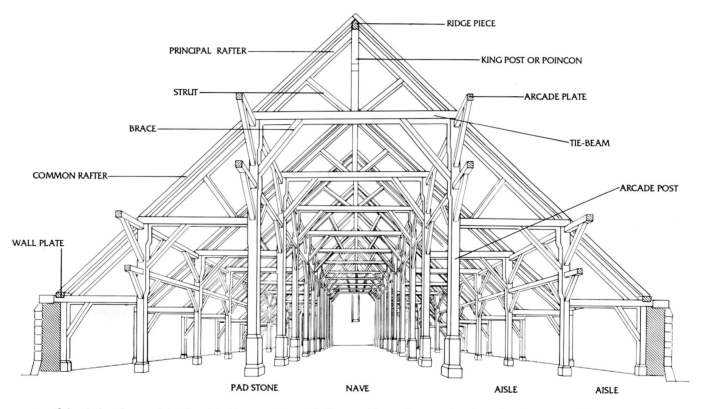

RIDGE PIECE

PRINCIPAL RAFTER

KING POST OR POINCON

STRUT

ARCADE PLATE

BRACE

TIE-BEAM

COMMON RAFTER

ARCADE POST

WALL PLATE

PAD STONE   NAVE   AISLE   AISLE

Components of the timber frame of the five-aisled barn at Parçay-Meslay near Tours, France. (See also color plate 7 and illustrations 3.1–3.5.)

PROLOGUE

The genesis of this book occurred one bright afternoon in 1987, when I stepped across the threshold of a deserted barn in upstate New York. The dim interior was reminiscent of a church and inspired the same sense of reverence. The central nave, actually a threshing floor made up of thick hemlock planks worn down by the passage of wagon wheels, communicated with the exterior through wide doors set in the end of the building. It was bound on either side by two rows of posts supporting the roof, which ran the full length of the structure and demarcated the aisles beyond.

Suspended from the lower portions of these posts were the remains of feeding racks, a reminder that the aisles had once served as stalls for cattle, oxen, and horses. Over my head huge beams, thicker than any I had ever seen before, spanned the threshing floor from post to post. Across these timbers a ceiling of poles had been laid, and wisps of hay dangling down between them betrayed the presence of a loft above in which crops had once been stored.

Such three-aisled barns, among the finest ever built in North America, were descended from farmhouses which had provided shelter for seventeenth-century Dutch and German immigrant families along with their livestock and harvest. Sometime later in the century, for reasons that can only be guessed at, the living quarters were split off as a separate dwelling. No farmhouses remain, but similar examples still survive in the Netherlands and northern Germany.

The earliest standing *hallenhaus,* as it is called in Lower Saxony, dates to the fifteenth century. Its evolution has been studied in more detail perhaps than any other rural building in Europe, owing to the patient work of Dutch and German archaeologists. What appeared to be its direct ancestors began turning up in the 1930s, as excavations of Bronze and Iron Age settlements unearthed the remains of a series of three-aisled houses now known to extend as far back as 1700 B.C.

From the twelfth century onward, and possibly well before then, aisled buildings were a common feature of the European landscape, serving not only as farmhouses but also as churches, infirmaries, feudal halls, market *halles,* and monastic barns. Walter Horn, a noted American architectural historian, believed they were descendants of Bronze Age archetypes.

If this was the case, then aisled dwellings should have been introduced to England by Anglo-Saxons who began migrating across from northern Germany in the fifth century A.D. But in fact no one can point with certainty to any site in England containing the remains of an aisled Saxon hall, although there were certainly contemporaneous aisled churches.

Aisled farmhouses have indeed been excavated in Britain, but they were Romano-British ones. After the Roman withdrawal they were gradually abandoned, and aisled buildings only reappeared in England with the Norman invasion of 1066. The great monastic barns that subsequently sprang up there on ecclesiastical estates must have originated in France, where they were already fully developed by the twelfth and thirteenth centuries, a period when the *hallenhaus* itself was still in its formative stages.

Recent archaeological discoveries have resolved some aspects of this puzzle by demonstrating that the fifteenth-century *hallenhaus* descended from a monospan farmhouse, to which aisles were subsequently added. Curiously, no traces of buildings from the twelfth to the fourteenth centuries have been found, which would help explain the final sequence of evolutionary steps that occurred.

Another riddle is the presence in the French countryside of three-aisled barns strikingly similar to the Dutch-built barns in New York. There is nothing to link them to building traditions in the Netherlands and Germany. Were they the result of independent evolution, or might they have diffused from a common source?

The answers to such questions lie in the centuries preceding the twelfth, a period about which there is frustratingly little information to go by. Documentary sources are sparse, and the fragments that survive relate to the Church and State rather than the everyday lives of the peasants. French archaeologists will undoubtedly come up with the evidence in due course, but it is presently lacking. The suggestions put forward here, therefore, are based partly on fact but also on speculation.

NOTE

In parts of Europe a barn is still regarded as a building solely for the storage of cereal crops, with cattle being housed in separate *byres* and horses in *stables*. Strictly speaking, this is the correct definition, for the original meaning of the word *barn* was "storeroom for barley" (from the Old Frisian *bere* for barley, and *aern* or *ern* for a storage place). Interestingly, Varro, the Roman agronomist, suggested that *horreum*, a word he frequently used to describe a granary, may have been derived from *hordeum*, the Latin for barley. He was probably mistaken. For the purposes of this book, however, the interpretation has been widened to include the American understanding of the term: an all-purpose building used for the storage of crops along with livestock.

The captions accompanying the photographs give the dimensions of the barns. Since these measurements vary from one source to another, they are not always entirely reliable.

SILENT SPACES
The Last of the Great Aisled Barns

1.1: The barn of Great Coxwell in Oxfordshire, England, belonged to the Cistercian abbey of Beaulieu and probably held the harvests taken off several of its outlying granges. Built around 1305, it measures 152 feet by 44 feet by 48 feet (46.3 m by 13.4 m by 14.6 m) to the ridge. The original entries were through the porches on either side, but in the eighteenth century larger doors were inserted at the ends to accommodate bigger wagons. The small door visible to the left provided access to a loft above the west porch for a granger, whose duty it was to watch over the contents of the barn (see also illustration 2.1). There is a dovecote in the east porch. An exterior shell of Cotswold stone protects the skeletal timber framework within.

Chapter 1
MULTIFUNCTIONAL BUILDINGS

Few have conveyed more eloquently the sense of reverence inspired within the dim and lofty spaces of an ancient barn than the young architect who wrote:

> They sheared in the Great Barn, called for the nonce the Shearing-barn, which on ground-plan resembled a church with transepts. It not only emulated the form of the neighbouring church of the parish, but vied with it in antiquity. Whether the barn had ever formed one of a group of conventual buildings nobody seemed to be aware: no trace of any such surroundings remained. The vast porches at the sides, lofty enough to admit a waggon laden to its highest with corn in the sheaf, were spanned by heavy-pointed arches of stone, broadly and boldly cut, whose very simplicity was the origin of a grandeur not apparent in erections where more ornament has been attempted. The dusky, filmed, chestnut roof, braced and tied in by huge collars, curves and diagonals, was far nobler in design, because more wealthy in material, than nine-tenths of those in our modern churches. Along each wall was a range of striding buttresses, throwing deep shadows on the spaces between them, which were perforated by lancet openings, combining in the proportions the precise requirements both of beauty and ventilation.
>
> One could say about this barn, what could hardly be said of either the church or the castle, akin to it in age and style, that the purpose which had dictated its original erection was the same with that to which it was still applied. Unlike and superior to either of those two typical remnants of medievalism, the old barn embodied practices which had suffered no mutilations at the hands of time. Here at least the spirit of the ancient builders was at one with the spirit of the modern beholder. Standing before this abraded pile, the eye regarded its present usage, the mind dwelt upon its past history, with a satisfying sense of functional continuity throughout—a feeling almost of gratitude, and quite of pride, at the permanence of the idea which had heaped it up. . . .
>
> Today the large side doors were thrown open towards the sun to admit a bountiful light to the immediate spot of the shearers' operations, which was a wooden threshing-floor in the centre, formed of thick oak, black with age and polished by the beating of flails for many generations, till it had grown as slippery and rich in hue as the stateroom floors of an Elizabethan mansion. Here the shearers knelt, the sun slanting in upon their bleached shirts, tanned arms, and the polished shears as they flourished, causing them to bristle with a thousand rays strong enough to blind a weak-eyed man. . . . So the barn was natural to the shearers, and the shearers were in Harmony with the barn.

THOMAS HARDY's *Far from the Madding Crowd* was published in 1874, when he was thirty-four, and the acclaim he received as a chronicler of English rural life eventually led him to abandon architecture altogether for a career as a novelist.

The parallel Hardy drew between barn and church is a relevant one. After all, Christian myth maintains that the very first house of worship had a manger for an altar, where the infant Jesus lay.

A three-aisled timber church excavated at St. Walburg in the Dutch

1.2

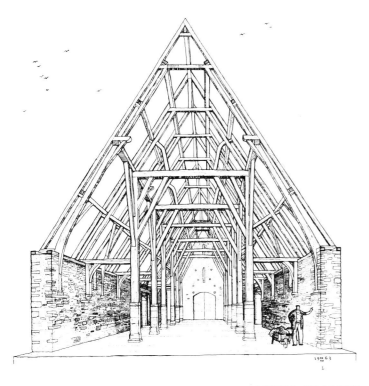

BARN, ABBEY GRANGE, GREAT COXWELL, BERKSHIRE, ENGLAND
VIEW LOOKING NORTHWARD

1.3

1.2–1.4: Six transverse frames divide the interior space of Great Coxwell into seven bays. Pairs of oak arcade posts 22.5 feet (7 m) tall and resting on stone bases about 7 feet high are connected transversely by tie-beams which, instead of surmounting the arcade plates as is customary in England (see illustrations 8.21 and 8.22), are here assembled in reverse. The two-tier roof system consists of an inner structure of truncated principal rafters supported by elbowed queen-struts to prevent them from sagging. Purlins lying horizontally across the backs of the principal rafters carry an outer layer of common rafters, which meet at their apex over a ridge piece. The intermediate trusses in the center of each bay are of cruck form up to the arcade plates, eliminating the need for additional pairs of arcade posts. The principal rafters above them are supported on small hammer-beams. Metal bolts indicate where repairs were made to the tie-beams in 1868.

1.4

1.5: Glastonbury Abbey barn is one of four surviving monospan barns that once belonged to the Benedictine monastery in Somerset, which at the time of the Norman Conquest was already the richest in England. It was built around 1375. The interior timber roof has a span of 33 feet (10 m). The wagon door in the end of the porch on the northwest side is surmounted by a window and the emblem of St. Luke. A smaller pedestrian door is visible to the right of it. Surmounting the buttresses at each of the four corners of the roof are the sculpted heads of benefactors of the abbey. The building is now part of the Somerset Rural Life Museum.

1.6: The sculpted head of a benefactor of Glastonbury adorns a corner of the abbey barn roof.

1.7: The magnificent interior of the unaisled tithe barn at Bradford-on-Avon in Wiltshire, which once belonged to the Benedictine nunnery of Shaftesbury. Built early in the fourteenth century, it has fourteen bays and measures 167.5 feet by 30.25 feet (51 m by 9 m). Wagon porches provide access to the fifth and tenth bays on the north side. Some of the roof trusses are two-tiered, with upper crucks resting on raised base crucks, while others are unbroken. (For a detail of the roof, see illustration 8.4.)

1.8: After passing through the doors in the porch of the tithe barn at Bradford-on-Avon, wagons were unloaded on the stone threshing floor in the foreground. During the threshing process (see color plate 5) low boards, or thresholds, were sometimes placed across the doorways to prevent the grain from spilling outside. When the grain was winnowed, doors on opposite sides of the barn were opened to create a draft of air that helped separate out the chaff.

1.10: A detail of the openings in the gable of the thirteenth-century Cistercian barn of Fourcheret, which stands on one of the granges of the Cistercian abbey of Chaalis, in Oise, France.

1.9: A winged bull, the emblem of St. Luke, decorates the gable over the window in the northwest porch of the Glastonbury Abbey barn.

1.11: Pilton, another of the barns of Glastonbury Abbey in Somerset, was built about 1375 to hold the harvest taken off 763 acres of *demesne* land. It measures 108.5 feet by 44 feet (33 m by 13.5 m). A fire in 1963 destroyed the ten timber roof trusses. The east gable is decorated with a winged man, the emblem of St. Matthew, and has a Tudor rose at its peak. The cross-pommée slit vents provided air circulation within the barn. (See also illustration 10.1.)

1.12–1.15: The elegant barn of the priory of Perrières in Calvados, Normandy, a dependency of the Benedictine abbey of Marmoutier at Tours, dates to the late twelfth or early thirteenth century. The six-bay building measures 98.5 feet by 57.5 feet (30 m by 17.5 m) overall. The central wagon door and the adjacent pedestrian door both open into a 26.5-foot-wide (8.5 m) nave. On either side rise five stone piers with decorated capitals, connected by Gothic arches. The king-post roof trusses have been rebuilt and a recently added interior wall partitions the space in half. (See also 9.5 and 9.6.)

I.13

23

city of Groningen, which dated perhaps to the early eleventh century, had a ground plan virtually identical to that of local barns of the period. Dutch Catholics, deprived of their churches in the Zaan region in the late sixteenth century, held their services in barns, and after their rights were restored in 1815 they continued to use these barn-churches, or erected new churches on the same site. The practice of worshiping in barns is maintained by the Amish in Pennsylvania today (see also illustration 6.13).[1]

The early twelfth-century Cistercian grange in France was a multi-purpose building that sheltered not only livestock, crops, and farm equipment, but also the lay brothers and presumably an oratory. Pilgrims and passing travelers were assured of a welcome within its walls.[2] The fifteenth-century Augustinian barn of Canteloup, disassembled in 1967 and moved to the Benedictine abbey of St. Wandrille near Rouen in Normandy, now serves as a splendid chapel, betraying no hint to the casual visitor of its former purpose.[3] Conversely, the Eglise Saint-Pierre à Doullens, east of Abbeville in France, was at some point transformed into an impressive barn, complete with hayloft above the nave.[4]

When it no longer had a congregation to serve, the ancient seventh-century Saxon chapel of St. Peter-on-the-Wall at Bradwell, in Essex, England, was resurrected as a barn (see illustration 4.1), and the refectory of the twelfth-century priory of St. Martin at Dover underwent a similar conversion. In 1283 the barn at Acton Burnell in Shropshire acted as a temporary House of Parliament when members were summoned there by Edward I.[5]

In southern Germany the Bauhofscheune (see illustration 7.6), an aisled municipal granary with a roof of churchlike complexity, built c. 1441 at Windsheim in Franconia, has been aptly described as "like the French market hall . . . nothing but a rural barn transplanted into the city."[6]

In addition to serving as a place of worship, Walter Horn noted, the aisled building in medieval Europe was used interchangeably as a

dwelling for the farmer, accommodating, often under a single roof, both his family and his cattle [see illustrations 6.9–6.11].

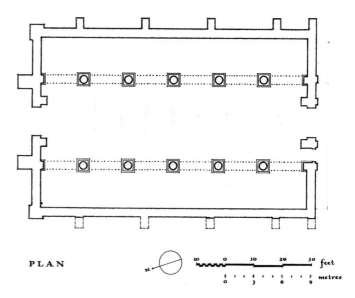

PLAN

PRIORY BARN, PERRIERES, CALVADOS, FRANCE

1.14

Used as a barn, it stored the harvest. In medieval England it became a standard form for rural manor halls and, on higher social levels, even for royal audience halls [see illustration 9.7]. It reached its peak of constructional beauty, both in England and on the Continent, in the great monastic tithe barns . . . and it was used in France from the twelfth century onward as the standard form of urban market halls. It was thus a building type known to everyone in the transalpine territories of medieval Europe."[7]

The Roman *basilica*, which dates back to the second century B.C., was equally versatile. Contrary to popular belief it could be either aisled or monospan, and served not only as an imperial audience hall, but also as a court of justice, stock exchange, or market-hall. It was because of its official association that the aisled basilica was adopted by Christians as the appropriate building for their place of worship.[8]

1.15

On Romano-British and Gallo-Roman villas, there were buildings of basilican plan by the third century A.D., sometimes containing a dwelling space at one end and crops or livestock at the other.[9]

At the risk of confusing the reader still further, barns belonging to medieval monasteries were referred to as *horrea*. To the Romans, however, *horrea* were not merely barns or granaries, but buildings where other objects might also be stored, such as farm tools on a villa, or equipment for troops on a military campaign. Like the basilica, the *horreum* too could be aisled or unaisled. Indeed in great cities like Rome it bore closer resemblance to a warehouse, with rows of rooms opening onto a porticoed courtyard. Elsewhere it might be built directly on the ground or elevated above it on piers to permit air circulation under the floor.[10]

This book covers some of the few remaining aisled *horrea* on monastic estates, the oldest of which may have been built in the twelfth century. They are instantly recognizable as barns, both in function and plan, but in attempting to trace their origins it is well to bear in mind that their prototypes may have been less clearly defined.

1.16

1.16–1.18: The feudal hall of Oakham Castle in Rutland is one of the finest examples left in England. The interior, which differs little today from an engraving made in the nineteenth century, bears a striking resemblance to the barn of the priory of Perrières in Normandy. Built by Walkelin de Ferrers soon after 1180, it originally stood on a motte (mound) defended by a ditch and wood tower. The two stone arcades are each made up of three piers joined by Romanesque arches. The capitals of the columns are decorated with acanthus foliage, above which are seated the headless figures of musicians. The sculpture resembles that of the choir at Canterbury Cathedral, begun in 1175 by French master mason William of Sens. The walls are decorated with symbolic horseshoes, traditionally surrendered to the lord of the manor by visiting peers of the realm. The roof was restored in 1621 and again in more recent times.

1.17

1.18

1.19, 1.20: The half-timbered parish church of St. James and St. Paul, Cheshire, was founded in 1343. Traces of fourteenth-century paintings are visible on the west wall of the nave.

1.21: The aisled market-hall of St. Pierre-sur-Dives in Calvados, Normandy, dates to the thirteenth or fourteenth century. Its interior dimensions are 225 feet by 64 feet (68.5 m by 19.5 m) and it stands 42 feet (13 m) high at the ridge. The roof was shelled during World War II by retreating Germans, and was subsequently restored. Similar market-halls or *halles,* both aisled and unaisled, were established in Paris during the twelfth century and were rented by guilds whose members dealt in such commodities as meat, fish, grain, wool, cloth, and shoes.

1.22: The French market-hall at Méréville (Essonne) was built in 1512 by Bertrand de Reilhac, a local lord, who established four annual fairs in addition to the weekly markets. His income came from levying taxes and renting out stalls to merchants from the region. The ten-bay building is 134.5 feet by 56.5 feet by 44.5 feet high (41 m by 17 m by 13.5 m). In such *halles* the aisles are occupied by merchants, leaving shoppers to browse unimpeded in the nave, while in a church the congregation is seated in the nave and the aisles usually provide the necessary access. Aisled buildings thus facilitate the flow of traffic.

2.1: The nine-bay barn at Bredon, built by the bishop of Worcester around 1344, measures 132 feet by 44 feet (40 m by 13.5 m). The further of the two wagon porches in its side contains a lodging for the granger, reached by covered exterior stairs. His room was furnished with a fireplace, while a door at the rear led into a gallery overlooking the interior, from where he could direct the unloading of the wagons, oversee the threshing and winnowing of the grain, and keep a tally of the harvest. The roof was badly damaged by fire in 1980.

Chapter 2
FEAST OR FAMINE

CIVILIZATION ORIGINATED with the discovery of grain. Where the seed sprouted, so too did human settlement. Cooperation was required to harvest and store it, government to ensure its equitable distribution, and writing to record its quantities and movements. Those gaining control of the supply became the ruling elite. In short, grain has been far more critical to human survival than oil, that lifeblood of the industrialized West.[1]

Granaries, which date back to the eighth millennium B.C. at sites along the headwaters of the Tigris River, enabled communities to draw upon reserves not only during the unproductive months, but also through more extended periods of crop failure and famine. Grain was consumed primarily in the form of bread, beer, and gruel.[2]

Famine destroyed the first great empire, that of the Akkadians of Mesopotamia, some 4,300 years ago. A drought lasting three centuries devastated farmlands to the north, driving the survivors to cities in the south, despite the erection of a 110-mile-long wall designed to keep many of them out. Lacking sufficient food and water to cope with the influx, the empire collapsed.[3]

Granaries were so crucial to survival that they were often built within fortified enclosures. However, such precautions failed to save the Athenians. During a siege in 87–86 B.C. their reserves ran out, and they were finally reduced to licking the skins of animals they had devoured. After Sulla's troops broke into the city, "in many houses they found human flesh prepared for food."[4]

Two thousand years ago Rome had a population of one million, a figure unequaled by any northern European city until the early nineteenth century.[5] Since cereals rather than meat formed the mainstay of its diet, some 40 million *modii* (about 294,000 tons)[6] had to be shipped annually to the capital. Increasingly, supplies and slaves to work the land had to be sought from conquered territories. Sicily and Sardinia were taken in the third century B.C., North Africa (present-day Tunisia) fell the next century, and Egypt followed in 30 B.C. Egypt provided a third of Rome's needs, and North Africa was richer still.

To feed Rome and its army of four hundred thousand men eventually required the resources of a huge empire that stretched from Egypt in the south to Scotland in the north, and the exaction of tributes from conquered tribes. It also entailed a navy to secure the safe passage of ships transporting grain to the capital. In 67 B.C. Pompey was given command of a fleet of five hundred vessels to eliminate piracy upon the cargo vessels, after which the price of grain dropped dramatically.[7]

The Republic, following the example of Athens a century earlier, had already established a regular food supply system by the third century B.C. Private individuals and families were responsible for the procurement of grain and financed the construction of *horrea,* or granaries, in which to store it. During crises they profited by hoarding and raising prices. On the other hand, when there were severe famines, citizen unrest obliged them to release supplies until the emergency had passed.

Some of these granaries were immense. The Horrea Galbana contained 140 rooms covering an area of 225,000 square feet (almost 21,000 square meters), almost two hundred times larger than the average 30-by-40-foot barn in New England. As protection against fire granaries were built of brick or blocks of *tufa.*[8]

In 123 B.C. the tribune Gaius Gracchus instituted monthly rations of cheap grain to an estimated 320,000 citizens of Rome and ordered the building of state *horrea* as a buffer against poor harvests and

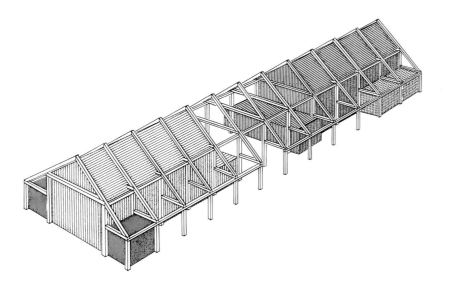

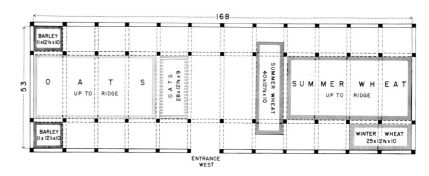

2.2: The twelfth-century Domesday of St. Paul's in London lists the contents of an aisled barn on the Manor of Adulvesnasa belonging to the cathedral. The description of this barn at Walton contains sufficient detail to show where and how the crops were stored within it. The building measured 168 feet by 53 feet (51 m by 16 m), with 21.5 feet of clearance under the tie-beam and 12 feet above. The oats, which take up much of the available space, were used to feed the workhorses on the farm.

disruptions in delivery. The distributions continued despite periodic disputes over the costs, and efforts to reduce or eliminate them.

Ultimately a compromise was reached whereby a dole of free grain was provided to fewer resident citizens, and many of the granaries remaining in private hands came under imperial ownership. By the third century A.D. bread was being handed out in place of grain, an indication of its vital importance in the diet.[9] One bakery reportedly consumed 50,000 pounds (22,680 kilograms) of flour daily.[10]

The towns and villas built by Romans occupying northwestern Europe had been amply provisioned with storehouses, as well as with an efficient network of waterways and roads for the distribution of food during emergencies. But when the legions departed in the fifth century, the infrastructure broke down. With the collapse of central authority many townspeople fled to rural areas, where they became vassals, protected by powerful landlords whom they relied upon to sustain them in times of crisis.[11]

Drought, flood, pestilence, and warfare resulted in recurring food shortages, particularly for the poor, who had meager reserves of grain, if any, to fall back on. Gregory, Bishop of Tours, in his *History of the Franks*, described the desperate struggle of peasants in Gaul faced with famine in 585 A.D.: "Many . . . gathered grasses and ate them, with the result that they swelled up and died. . . . The merchants took sad advantage of the people, selling a bushel of corn or a half measure of wine for the third of a gold piece. The poor sold themselves into slavery in order to obtain something to eat."[12]

Under the emperor Constantine (313–336 A.D.) Christianity became the State religion, and when the State crumbled, the Church assumed responsibility for the food distributions. Its villas in Sicily and North Africa continued to ship produce to the city. In November 590 A.D., the papal *horrea* were destroyed along with several thousand bushels of wheat when the Tiber flooded its banks. In 605 A.D. Pope Sabinianus was criticized for auctioning grain which had been intended for the poor.[13]

This practice of feeding the needy continued under Charlemagne's rule in the eighth and ninth centuries. Bread and ale were arguably the two most important components of the medieval diet. Frequently referred to as the staff of life, white bread was reserved for the upper classes, while darker varieties were given to the poor. The ale, which was also made from grain, had the consistency of soup. The peasants supplemented this with a pottage of oats, peas, and beans. Meat, when available, came from game or domestic beasts like pigs that foraged in the woods, but monks were forbidden to eat it unless they were sick.

The monasteries gained a reputation for charity, providing hospitality and shelter to travelers and pilgrims, distributing bread, clothing, and alms to the poor, and caring for the sick in their infirmaries. None of this would have been possible had not the monks, like the Romans before them, constructed storehouses and stockpiled grain and other provisions to carry them through the lean periods.

Adelhard, the abbot of Corbie in France, issued a set of directives in 822 stipulating that "loaves be given out every day at the poorhouse—forty-five made from three and a half pounds of maslin [a mixture of wheat and rye] and five made of wheat or spelt such as the vassals receive, making a total of fifty loaves," along with a half modius of beer and additional rations of cheese, bacon, vegetables, and eels.[14] Another monastery, St. Riquier, reportedly fed four hundred needy people daily. Later Cluny made a practice of distributing 250 salt pork carcasses each Lent.[15]

Under the feudal system of medieval Europe, most of the food supplies were controlled by the nobility and Church. No matter how hard the peasants toiled on their own meager holdings and on the *demesnes* of their landlords, the hierarchy appropriated up to half their income through tithes, rents, and other obligations. They were unable to produce significant surpluses of their own to store away for emergencies, and indeed often were left with barely enough to survive on.

The landholdings of the Church were vast. For example, during the Carolingian period the monastery of Lorsch in central Germany held estates that stretched from the Netherlands to Switzerland. The monks raised cereals, vines, and livestock in those areas best suited to support them. Crops devastated by flood or drought in one region might be spared in another. Farming on such a scale must have called for substantial barns, no doubt several on each particular estate.

During the early ninth century the abbey of St. Germain-des-Pres in the Ile-de-France possessed about 81,000 acres (32,748 hectares), tended by around 13,300 peasants and their families. Along with a further 160 serfs and laymen attached to the monastery itself, this meant in effect that each of the 120 monks was supported by 112 peasants.[16]

Compared with present-day cereal yields of 20:1 and higher, those of the Carolingian period averaged an abysmal 2:1 or less, rising by the thirteenth century to around a paltry 4:1 for wheat on the bishop of Winchester's estates in England.[17] Since the author of a thirteenth-century treatise on husbandry declared that a 5:1 yield for wheat was normal, perhaps these low returns took into account losses from pests and spoilage, or the amounts distributed to servants and workers in payment for their labor.[18]

One reason was that the land lacked fertilizer. With cereals forming the bulk of the daily diet, the emphasis on arable farming resulted in insufficient pastureland, and the consequent scarcity of livestock meant a dearth of manure for the fields. On occasion peasants were obliged to present a pot of dung to their landlords, which gives some indication of its value.

To compound the problem, the population began rising dramatically between the eleventh and thirteenth centuries. There were an estimated sixty-seven million inhabitants in all of Europe in 200 A.D., but by 700 A.D. their number had fallen to twenty-seven million. By 1300, however, the populace had climbed back up to seventy-three million. This growth was accompanied by increasing land clearances to meet the demand for food. As had occurred under the Roman occupation, agricultural surpluses were produced in sufficient quantity to encourage people to move to the towns. Flourishing markets led to even greater demands for food, and the burgeoning economy stimulated further population growth, which in turn led to intensified exploitation of the land.[19]

Forests cleared by swiddening, or slashing and burning, might result in crop yields as high as 20:1 initially, but such temporary bursts of productivity were deceptive and unsustainable. Agrarian practices were ecologically unsound, as nutrient reserves were transferred from uncropped areas to sustain the arable fields. The wheat monoculture resulted in the spread of soil pathogens. Repeated plowings were beneficial in the short term but contributed ultimately to the leaching of minerals from the soil.[20]

There were recurring food shortages throughout the Middle Ages. Ralph Glaber, a Cluniac monk, described in graphic detail the awful famine of 1032–1034, after three consecutive harvests had been ruined by the rains:

> Many people who moved . . . to flee the famine, and who had found hospitality on the way, were murdered in the night, and served as food for those who had welcomed them. . . . Bodies of the dead were in many places torn out of the ground and equally served to appease hunger . . . in the region of Mâcon . . . people took out of the ground a white soil which looked like

clay, mixed it with what flour or bran they had, and made out of this mixture loaves with which, they reckoned, they would not die of hunger . . . the human voice itself became thin, like the little cries of dying birds.[21]

The benevolent bishop of Paderborn in Westphalia had two shiploads of grain brought from Cologne to his diocese during a crisis in 1025. But a century later Charles the Good, Count of Flanders, had to

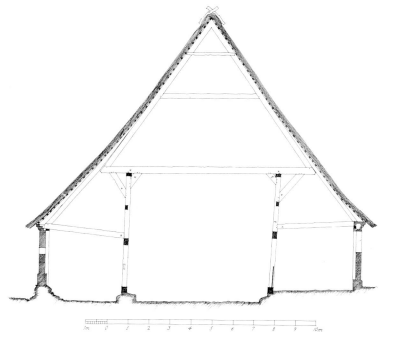

2.3: A cross section of the barn at Skaføgard in Djursland, Denmark, dating from 1579. As at Ardenne in Normandy (see 2.5, 2.6) the nave floor is sunk below the level of the wagon passage in the side aisle.

intervene directly to compel collegiate churches and monasteries to open their tithe barns and sell grain to the citizens at a fair price.[22]

Paintings of the period depict peasants deformed and handicapped by constant malnutrition. The legend of the Pied Piper who enticed away the children of Hameln instead of its rats, allegorizes a desire to rid cities of the hungry and homeless. Large numbers of people suffered convulsions and hallucinations from ergotism, caused by a poisonous fungus growing on rye. Average life expectancy was a mere twenty-four to thirty years.[23]

These hardships were but a prelude to the terrible events of the fourteenth century. From about 750 to 1230 A.D. there had been a warming trend in the climate, and the mild temperatures, comparable to those of the twentieth century, may have been related to the great land clearances and increase in food production. However, by the middle of the thirteenth century, agrarian expansion had halted, alpine glaciers began to advance for the first time since the eighth century, and the climate turned ominously colder and wetter.[24]

During the decade from 1310 to 1320 there was continuous flooding. A single bad harvest affected peasants more than higher social classes, because they had little to fall back on, but repeated crop failures like those of 1315 and 1316 proved disastrous for the rich as well. In 1315 fields belonging to the bishop of Winchester in England yielded insufficient seed for the following year's crop, which yielded still less, about half the normal amount. The mud was so thick it

2.4: The ten-bay barn belonging to the Cistercian abbey of Froidmont (Oise) in Picardy, constructed in the thirteenth century, measures 115 feet by 53 feet (35 m by 16.2 m). The wagons passed down the east aisle, and crops were stacked up on the floor of the far aisle and nave. In terms of actual volume devoted to the storage of the harvest this is the most efficient utilization of space, although it is more labor intensive than if the sheaves were unloaded on either side of a central passage down the nave. Presumably labor was still cheap and plentiful when the barn was first built. Tragically it now lies abandoned, and the roof has collapsed. (See also color plate 28.)

2.5: The Premonstratensian abbey of Notre-Dame d'Ardenne, in Calvados, Normandy, was founded in 1121. The nine-bay barn, built in the thirteenth century, measures 157.5 feet by 52.5 feet (48 m by 16 m). The roof was destroyed by artillery fire during the Normandy invasion in 1944 and has since been rebuilt. Each arcade is made up of eight stone piers linked by Gothic arches. One aisle is wider than the other and served as the wagon passage. The nave floor is sunk slightly below the level of this aisle, perhaps to gain additional storage space. A pedestrian door opening in one side provided access to a transverse threshing floor, while a window opposite it created the necessary cross-draft of air for winnowing. There was a lookout at the apex of the far gable, accessible by stairs leading up the slope of the gable wall.

sucked the shoes from the oxen, the ground so sodden it was near impossible to plow. The hay remained waterlogged. The price of wheat tripled in the city.[25]

In Kent, a third of all thefts in 1316–17 involved food. Peasants, unable to buy even seed grain, were reduced to eating cats and dogs. Unscrupulous bakers augmented their flour with the droppings of pigs and pigeons.[26] Throughout Europe the decade produced the worst famines of the past millennium, with mortality rates as high as 15 percent. Guards at the market in Florence were given orders to chop off the hands and feet of rioters. Troops were posted at gibbets in Mainz, Cologne, and Strasbourg to prevent ravenous mobs from tearing corpses from the gallows.[27]

Weakened and impoverished, Europe's agony became a catastrophe when in 1347 Italian merchants trading with the Orient sailed their ships into Genoa and Pisa. Flea-infested rats carried bubonic plague to the cities, and the Black Death spread northward like wildfire. The rats took shelter in the thatched roofs of peasant houses, encouraging the rapid spread of the disease.

When the Black Death ended in 1351, an estimated twenty-four million people, one-third of all living in Europe, had died. But just as recovery seemed at hand the nightmare returned. A second epidemic

2.6: A pre–World War II view of the interior of the barn shows the nave filled with hay and a threshing machine standing in the wider of the two aisles. The bases of the stone piers have been worn away from centuries of contact with the axles of wagon wheels.

erupted in 1361, killing a further 10 to 20 percent of the population. The cycle was repeated in 1369, and on and off again every four to twelve years up to the sixteenth century. By 1430 the European population was perhaps two-thirds less than it had been in 1290.[28]

The Black Death made no distinctions between its victims, consuming the aristocracy, clergy, and craftsmen as readily as it did the peasants. But even before it struck, the idealism of the twelfth century had begun to yield to disillusionment. Ultimately it was the accumulated wealth of the monasteries that led to their undoing. Members of the Church hierarchy had not only come from aristocratic families, they lived in comparable luxury too. Faith in the Church itself and the clergy waned, although people still sought salvation in other forms of religion.[29]

Monasteries became less committed to feeding the poor. In England Bolton Priory, which had given 2 percent of its income to charity immediately prior to the famine of 1315–1318, spent only one-tenth of this by the end. In 1506 the bishop of Lincoln's contribution consisted of spoiled fish.[30]

Ironically, the peasants who survived the horrors of famine and the plague emerged better off. Changes already under way late in the thirteenth century were accelerated by the events of the fourteenth. Infertile land was abandoned, and only the better fields kept in cultivation. The soil had an opportunity to recover. Deprived of its labor force, the manorial system went into decline. The aristocracy maintained possession of its estates but could no longer enforce the old feudal obligations.

Peasants were released from serfdom and were able to move and rent land where they wished. Although less land was being farmed, the population had declined even further, so that they were able to increase the size of their holdings. They no longer feared starvation. For the first time, they could accumulate and hold on to their agrarian

surpluses. In England both landlords and their tenants invested in barns built by professional carpenters. They typically measured 30 to 45 feet long by 15 feet wide and sometimes incorporated timbers taken from abandoned buildings.[31]

To the pioneers who arrived in the New World in the seventeenth century the barn was the most indispensable of farm buildings, a shelter for both crops and livestock against the bitter North American winter. Michel-Guillaume St. Jean de Crèvecoeur, a Frenchman who settled in New York State around the time of the Revolutionary War, observed that "the barn, with regard to its situation, size, convenience, and good finishing, is an object, in the mind of a farmer, superior even to that of his dwelling. Many don't care much how they are lodged, provided that they have a good barn and barn-yard, and indeed it is the criterion by which I always judge of a farmer's prosperity. On this building he never begrudges his money." The pioneer family was prepared to wait as long as nine harvests before erecting a permanent house. "If all the new settlers acted as prudently," de Crèvecoeur added, "misfortune would occur less frequently among them."[32]

Up to the second half of the nineteenth century a greater percentage of the populations of Europe and North America was engaged in the cultivation of land than in any other industry. For them, as for those Mesopotamian communities of the eighth millennium B.C., food reserves stored in barns and granaries were critical to human survival.

Tragically, the decline of traditional agriculture in the twentieth century has led to the decay and destruction of untold numbers of barns. "They stand abandoned, like great sailing ships stranded in a world where there is no more wind," lamented one American writer.[33] Silent tombs pulsing with the ghosts of ancestors, their passing marks the severance of our own ties to the land.

Chapter 3

MONASTERIES AND THE LEGACY OF ROME

THE LEGACY of Rome lingered on in northwestern Europe, long after the legions themselves departed at the start of the fifth century A.D. It included such enduring features as the Latin language and classical texts, administration and social organization, art and architecture, education and law, coinage, weights and measures, roads and towns, taxation and tithes, an emphasis on bread and wine both in the daily diet and in Christian ritual, water mills and other forms of technology, the villa system of agricultural exploitation, the transformation of native peoples into peasants and slaves, and, most important, Christianity itself. It now fell to the Church to perpetuate the traditions of the Mediterranean world.[1]

Monasteries were to be its principal agents until the twelfth century. At the start of the sixth century the Frankish ruler Clovis had converted to Christianity. He forged an alliance with the Church, not only bringing it under his royal protection but encouraging it to maintain its cultural ties to Rome.

Under Clovis the Franks had assumed control of most of Roman-held Gaul, with the exception of Provence. Surprisingly, they probably accounted for no more than 5 percent of the overall population, prompting historians to observe how small minorities can effect major changes on the populace at large.[2] This surely also applies to the subsequent impact the monasteries themselves had on rural communities.

The Frankish empire reached its zenith under the rule of Charlemagne (769–814), who in the year 800 was proclaimed Holy Roman Emperor in Rome by Pope Leo III. During his reign monasteries became by far the most important administrative, spiritual, cultural, educational, and economic centers in Europe. Their dominance began to fade during the twelfth century, when schools were founded in the towns, but with the rise of the Cistercian order they remained the leading agricultural power for some time to come.[3] Their leaders were often of noble birth, and a few were related to Charlemagne himself, such as his cousin Adelhard, abbot of Corbie.

The monastic movement in Gaul was launched by the son of a Roman soldier, St. Martin, who in 360–361 established a cell at a Gallo-Roman villa near Poitiers. Once it took root it sprouted numerous daughterhouses in the fifth and sixth centuries.[4]

Another saint of Roman descent, Benedict of Nursia (c. 480–553), founded an abbey at Monte Cassino between Rome and Naples. Here he formulated a set of statutes which later attracted Charlemagne's attention. Charlemagne ordered all monasteries within his empire to adopt the Benedictine Rule, which would be the leading influence up to the close of the eleventh century, when the Cistercian order was instituted.

St. Augustine was sent from Rome by Pope Gregory the Great to establish the first Benedictine settlement at Canterbury, England, in 597. From here the missionaries Willibrord and Boniface set out to convert the Saxons, Frisians, Thuringians, and other native tribes of the eastern Frankish kingdom in the late seventh and early eighth centuries. The monastery of Echternach (c. 700) was founded by Willibrord at a site where there had previously been a Roman villa of palatial dimensions.[5]

Viollet-le-Duc, the French architectural theorist, was among the first to suggest that monasticism sprang up on the foundations of Roman villas, and that villas had a direct influence on monastic planning up to the eleventh century.[6] The earliest square cloister known belongs to the monastery of Lorsch, instituted between 765 and 774. According to the archaeologist who excavated the site, it was originally the villa of a Frankish nobleman modeled after a Roman *villa rustica,* before being converted to monastic use.[7]

The collapse of the Empire did not result in a universal destruction of the Roman infrastructure. If one accepts the accounts of Sidonius Apollinarius, written at his villa at Clermont-Ferrand later in the fifth century, life continued very much as before in parts of Gaul. Several tribes, including a number of Franks, had already settled peacefully amongst the Romans and had even served as auxiliary troops in defense of the Empire. As successful participants in the Roman administrative and political system they had become increasingly more civilized in their outlook and had little desire to regress to their former tribal customs.[8]

Villas varied enormously in their scale and plan. The ones appropriated by the Frankish nobility in all likelihood had belonged to affluent Romans and Gallo-Romans and were run in similar manner to those of Italy. Such estates were often tripartite in nature, consisting of a manor, or *villa urbana,* a working farm, the *villa rustica,* and storage buildings, the *villa fructuaria.* Property subsequently donated to the Church presumably consisted of estates, or parts of estates, such as these. Villas owned by less affluent individuals often combined all three elements into a single architectural unit.[9]

By the mid-ninth century some 1,254 monasteries had been established, many in or around Roman-built towns such as Paris, Le Mans, Tours, and Trier.[10] In Trier itself a Benedictine convent, known in 895 as the Monasterium S. Mariae vocatum Orrea, was constructed over

3.1

the remains of a pair of aisled fourth-century Roman *horrea,* or granaries.[11]

Evidently the native populations lacked the Romans' skill in building with brick and stone, for numerous villas were eventually abandoned and transformed into religious shrines marked by cemeteries and chapels constructed of reused masonry. Every villa would have had its *horreum,* which, since it was designed for storage, could be readily converted into a house of worship. Other villas were preserved as manorial estates for centuries to come, but it is unclear how long the buildings themselves retained their original form.[12]

The Benedictine monastery of Cluny developed into the largest monastery ever built, controlling by the twelfth century some fifteen hundred abbeys and priories throughout Europe. It was established in 909 on a Gallo-Roman villa in Burgundy donated by William of Aquitaine. As was the customary practice of feudal lords, William and his wife, Ingelsborg, delivered "to the apostles Peter and Paul . . . [our] domain of Cluny, farm, oratories, slaves of both sexes, vineyards, fields, meadows, forests, waters, streams, mills, rights of passage, lands cultivated or uncultivated, without reserve . . . for the salvation of our souls and our bodies."[13]

The buildings may have resembled those on an estate belonging possibly to Charlemagne himself a century earlier at Annappes, near Lille in France. The *Brevium exempla,* an inventory taken around 812 A.D., reported: "We found on the royal estate of Annappes the royal hall very well constructed of stone, with three chambers, the entire house surrounded by a gallery with eleven heatable rooms . . . and below one *cellarium* [larder] . . . inside the courtyard seventeen

3.1–3.5: The early thirteenth-century barn at Parçay-Meslay is the last surviving five-aisled monastic barn in France. Behind the unusually broad gable lies a 33-foot-wide (10 m) nave, flanked on either side by twin aisles. (The Cistercian monastery of Clairvaux once owned a seven-aisled barn on its grange at Ultra Albam and another of six aisles on the original *monasterium vetus*.) The thirteen-bay barn measures 170.5 feet by 80 feet by 44 feet to the ridge (52 m by 24.5 m by 13.5 m). Its roof was rebuilt in the fifteenth century, possibly reusing some of the old timbers, after being set ablaze by the English in 1437. The timber framework stands independent of the masonry wall. None of the twelve aisled trusses line up with the exterior wall buttresses. As in England, each tie-beam and plate is assembled at the head of a jowled arcade post with a lap-dovetail joint (see 8.21–8.23). The *poinçon* (king post) carries both a ridge piece and a parallel subridge.

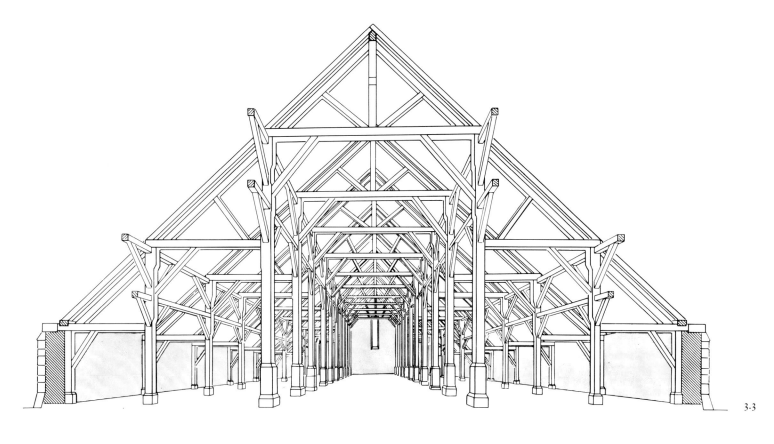

3.3

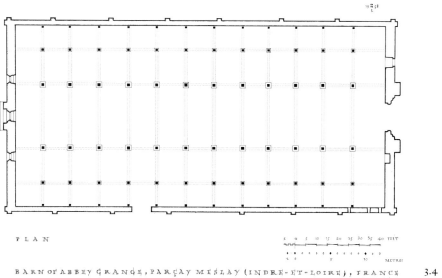

PLAN

BARN OF ABBEY GRANGE, PARÇAY MESLAY (INDRE-ET-LOIRE), FRANCE   3.4

3.5

3.6–3.11: Vaulerent (also known as Vaulerand, in Val-d'Oise), the longest monastic barn left in Europe, was one of fifteen outlying granges of the Cistercian abbey of Châalis. The abbey farmed 380 hectares (around 930 acres) of land here when the barn was built during the first half of the thirteenth century. Containing thirteen bays, it measures 236 feet by 75.5 feet by 67.5 feet high (72 m by 23 m by 20.6 m) and has a volume of 870,000 cubic feet. Its two rows of masonry arcades have Gothic pointed arches and stand 42.5 feet high. A spiral staircase in the circular tower leads to a space at the top from which the granger could observe the laborers while simultaneously keeping watch for impending danger. Halfway up the tower there is access to a ledge overlooking the interior of the barn. The original unbroken roof was destroyed sometime prior to 1446, perhaps during the wars with the English. When it was rebuilt, the rafters were shortened and set at a shallower angle to create a clerestory.

3.7

other houses built of timber [including] a stable, kitchen, bakehouse, two *spicaria* [granaries] and three *scuras* [barns]."[14] The facilities included many of the requirements of a medieval monastery.

There is nothing to indicate what the barns looked like or whether they were aisled (see page 42). But the details of the stone residence, with its gallery, eleven heatable rooms, and *cellarium,* suggest a villa laid out in the Roman tradition.[15] The cellar contained smoked carcasses of pigs, sausages, lard, and cheese. Inside the barns were cereals, beans, and peas from the previous year as well as the current one. Nearby were five water mills to grind flour for the landlord and peasants living in the vicinity.

The wealthy proprietors of the great villas of the Roman period

BARN OF THE ABBEY GRANGE OF VAULERAND, SEINE-ET-OISE, FRANCE

3.8

48

had exploited slave labor and dependent tenant farmers in order to sell their surpluses to nearby towns and military garrisons. Just how much Roman influence can be detected in the operation of monastic estates of the early medieval period is a matter still open to debate. When the Empire crumbled, so too did the towns, and there was no longer any incentive to produce surpluses for sale to them. Initially the Frankish elite seem to have been content to move from one villa to the next, living off the provisions garnered by their vassals.[16]

The sprawling monastic estates of the Carolingian period were still referred to as *villae,* but the lands attached to them now had assumed a bipartite division. The largest area, known as the *demesne,* typically might have a kitchen garden, fishpond, orchard, vineyard, arable fields for cereals, pastures for sheep and cattle, and extensive woodlands. All foodstuffs taken from the *demesne* belonged to the landlord.

The forests provided construction materials, firewood, and game for the proprietor, but the peasants were also permitted to let their pigs forage in them. The farm buildings, such as the dwellings, stables, workshops, and barns, were contained within a protective courtyard. The barns had to be substantial enough to hold both the grain harvested on the *demesne* fields and tithes owed by peasants.

The rest of the estate was parceled out between tenant farmers and slaves, who in return were obliged to cultivate the *demesne* land. Much of what they grew for themselves had to be handed over to the monastery, particularly in the form of tithes. The burdens placed on the slaves were more onerous than those placed on the free peasants. Other serfs lived on the grounds of the monastery, which was directly responsible for their care.

The payment of tithes, comprising one-tenth of the products taken from the land, dates back to the Old Testament. The Book of Deuteronomy (12:17) specified tithes of corn, wine, oil, and the firstborn of herds and flocks. The Romans had obtained grain from Sicily through annual tributes of tithes. By the fifth and sixth centuries the system had become accepted in northern Europe, and was made obligatory by Pepin the Short and Charlemagne in the eighth cen-

Color plate 1: The superb eighteenth-century barn at Østrupgaard, north of Faaborg in Denmark, also has a wagon passage in one side aisle. The building is approximately 197 feet long by 48 feet wide (60 m by 14.5 m).

Color plate 4: A Flemish manuscript of around 1500 illustrates peasants bearing sheaves into a barn.

Color plate 5: In another scene from the Luttrell Psalter, peasants thresh a sheaf with flails in order to separate out the ears of grain. The jointed flail was invented around the fifth century, allowing workers to stand fairly upright during the task. Although the Romans often threshed with an ox-drawn sled, they also used a simple staff, or *fustis,* which must have been extremely tiring to the back.

Color plate 6: The magnificent ruins of the Benedictine abbey of Jumièges, founded around 655 A.D. near Rouen in Normandy, evoke some idea of the grandeur and scale of a medieval monastery.

Color plate 7: The fortified grange built by Abbot Hugue de Rochecourbon (1211–1227) at Parçay-Meslay (Indre-et-Loire), was owned by the Benedictine abbey of Marmoutier in Tours. The courtyard, with its outbuildings and fishponds, is enclosed by a wall, and entry is gained via a monumental arched gateway surmounted by a two-story square tower. The manor house was destroyed in World War II. The long roof of the barn is visible on the left side of the grange.

Judging by the remarks of a visitor, Cistercian granges must have been just as impressive: "You would not suppose that these granges only serve as the dwellings of the lay brothers; you would take them for cloisters of monks, if the yokes of oxen, plows, and other implements fitted for rustic labor would not reveal the occupation of their inhabitants, and if you did not observe that no books are being opened there. For as relates to the buildings, you would say that it is suitable for a great convent of monks, both by sight, size, and beauty." (V. Mortet and P. Deschamps, *Recueil de textes relatifs à l'histoire de l'architecture en France au moyen âge, XIe–XIIe siècles*, Paris, 1929, pp. 27–29.)

Color plate 8: The barn (c. 1280) of the Cistercian abbey of Ter Doest at Lissewege in Belgium is sheathed in brick and rises on land drained by Cistercians in the twelfth and thirteenth centuries. The gables have blind Gothic arches. Measuring around 180 feet by 72 feet by 59 feet high (55 m by 22 m by 18 m), the carpentry of this barn is similar in some respects to that of Great Coxwell in England. (For other views of Ter Doest, see 9.8–9.10.)

Color plate 9: The Cistercian barn at Vaulerent is the longest monastic barn in Europe. The original roof had no clerestory. (See also 3.6–3.11.)

Color plate 10: A monospan field barn, with the date 1850 inscribed in the lintel above the door, at Masse (Aveyron), in the Rouergue. The lower level serves as a shelter for cattle. At the rear end an earthen ramp leads to a door opening into the loft above, which is used for storage of fodder. There are small ventilation openings under the eaves.

Color plate 11: A granary, or *espigueiro,* for the storage of maize near Covas in northern Portugal. Similar granaries in Spain are called *hórreo.*

Color plate 12: The Deertz barn after conversion to residential use
(see illustrations 6.2–6.8).

Color plate 13: The *helm,* or *rutenberg,* with its adjustable roof, was first
used for crop storage in the late Bronze Age. This example
is from Birsana, a village in the Mara-
mures region of Romania.

Color plate 14: An early eighteenth-century granary, or *speicher,* from the Gütersloh district, now in the collection of the open-air museum at Detmold in Westphalia, Germany.

Color plate 15: A pattern of timber and brick nogging decorates the gable of the manorial Münchhausen barn, built in 1561 and now part of the collection of the open-air museum at Cloppenburg in Lower Saxony.

Color plate 16: The late twelfth- or early thirteenth-century barn of the Benedictine priory of Perrières in Calvados, Normandy, is arguably the most serene and graceful of all surviving aisled barns (see 1.12–1.15).

Color plate 17: The 1750 farmhouse at Wulften, near Cloppenburg in Lower Saxony, has a fine, jettied gable overlooking the farmyard, in contrast with the plain gable of the dwelling at the other end.

Color plate 18: The all-timber Barley Barn, the oldest in England, was built during the first half of the thirteenth century by the Knights Templars on their manor at Cressing Temple in Essex. Nearby stands the Wheat Barn, erected later the same century. The Templars also owned the barn at the Commanderie de St.-Vaubourg, at Val-de-la-Haye in Normandy (9.2–9.4). After the order was suppressed in 1312, the property was turned over to the Hospitallers.

Color plate 19: The impressive oak frame of the twelve-bay barn at Harmondsworth was raised in 1426–27 and is 191 feet (58 m) long. It replaced another barn on the same site. The manor, belonging originally to St. Catherine's Abbey near Rouen in Normandy, was purchased in 1390 by William of Wykeham, Bishop of Winchester, to endow his new college.

Color plate 21: A bridled anchor-beam assembly in the barn (c. 1400) of the Manoir de la Cour du Mont at Duclair (Seine-Maritime) in Normandy. The manor was a dependency of the Benedictine abbey of Jumièges.

Color plate 20: A detail of the joinery at the head of the post supporting the hipped roof of Méréville.

Color plate 22: Scarf-joints are used to connect short timbers end to end to make longer members. Because they overlap one another, such joints indicate the sequence in which the timbers were originally assembled. This splayed scarf with key is in the arcade plate of the fourteenth-century barn at Frindsbury in Kent. (For an example of a *trait-de-Jupiter* scarf, see 4.10.)

Color plate 23: The thirteenth-century Grange aux Dimes (tithe barn) at Heurteauville (Seine-Maritime) in Normandy belonged to the Benedictine abbey of Jumièges (see color plate 6). It has a thatched roof and measures 91 feet by 56 feet (27.65 m by 17 m). There is a central wagon entry into the nave and a pedestrian door just visible in the left sidewall.

Color plate 24: The triangular roof truss of the thirteenth-century Grange aux Dimes at Heurteauville consists of two principal rafters tenoned at their feet to a horizontal tie-beam. They support a vertical *poinçon* carrying a ridge piece. Horizontal purlins lie on cleats attached to the backs of the principals, and the common rafters resting over them create a two-tier roof system. The collar above the tie-beam prevents the principal rafters from sagging. Angled struts to it from the *poinçon* serve to reduce any twisting effect, while a second pair of struts to the ridge piece counteracts longitudinal racking.

Color plate 25: The timber arcade posts of the five-bay barn are supported on pad stones. The bridled anchor-beam, or *kopbalken*, in the foreground has been reinforced by a pair of beams which straddle the arcade plates and clasp the *poinçon* and principal rafters (see detail in 8.5).

Color plate 26: The tower at Masse (Aveyron) in the Rouergue was built in 1453 by the Cistercian abbey of Bonneval. The Rouergue and Aquitaine were ceded to the English in 1360 during the Hundred Years War, and the countryside was thereafter pillaged by mercenaries. As a result fortified stone towers were erected to accommodate the grangers, seed grain, and provisions for the workers. After the fighting ended in 1453 a number of granges were converted into residences. Although it has a grain chute in its rear wall, the tower at Masse may have been intended more as an abbot's residence.

Color plate 27: Stone walls protected the thirteenth-century grange of Gaussan (Aude) belonging to the Cistercian abbey of Fontfroide near Narbonne. Within the compound is a twelfth-century chapel, the former lodgings of the lay brothers, a fourteenth-century tower, stables, and a wine *cellier*.

Color plate 28: The monastic barns of medieval Europe have never been surpassed in scale or beauty. The Cistercians alone constructed an estimated ten to twenty thousand of them. Today just a handful remain. The roof of this magnificent thirteenth-century barn, erected by the Cistercian abbey of Froidmont in Picardy, has collapsed and is too costly to restore (see also 2.4). Mourning the passing of such splendid buildings, the American writer Curtis Stadtfeld lamented, "They stand abandoned, like great sailing ships stranded in a world where there is no more wind."

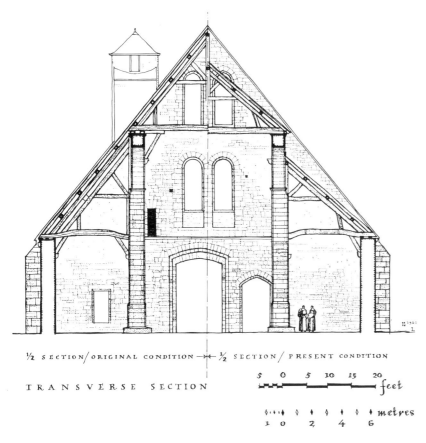

½ SECTION/ORIGINAL CONDITION — ½ SECTION/PRESENT CONDITION

TRANSVERSE SECTION

5 0 5 10 15 20
feet

metres
1 0 2 4 6

BARN OF THE ABBEY GRANGE OF VAULERAND
SEINE·ET·OISE, FRANCE

3.9

tury. In 822 Abbot Adelhard of Corbie noted that tithes owed to the monastery by its dependents included grain, vegetables, wine, livestock, and milk.[17]

The peasants were required to take their sheaves to the monastic tithe barns where, during the cold, dark winter months, they laboriously flailed and winnowed the grain (see color plates 4 and 5). Because the monastery was immobile, all the victuals necessary for its sustenance had to be transported from the various estates and stored either in its *cellarium* (larder), or in a large *horreum* (barn) or *granarium* (granary) within the precincts. At one point Corbie had 140

servants whose sole duties were to bring provisions to the monks.[18] Surplus produce was sold off or kept in anticipation of unforeseen emergencies the following season.

Whether Roman agrarian techniques were practiced on monastic estates is not entirely clear. Agriculture has a long and conservative history. Iron Age tribespeople had been successful farmers prior to their conquest by Caesar.[19] The imposition of corn taxes on them to feed the occupying armies undoubtedly brought some changes, along with the villa system of production. Many of the soldiers were themselves part-time farmers, and Augustus settled colonies of vet-

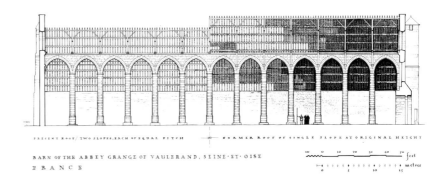

PRESENT ROOF/ TWO SLOPES, EACH OF EQUAL PITCH ——— FORMER ROOF OF SINGLE SLOPE AT ORIGINAL HEIGHT

BARN OF THE ABBEY GRANGE OF VAULERAND, SEINE·ET·OISE
FRANCE

10 0 10 20 30 40 50 feet
0 5 10 15 metres

3.10

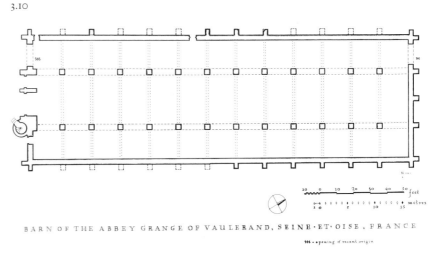

BARN OF THE ABBEY GRANGE OF VAULERAND, SEINE·ET·OISE, FRANCE

— opening of recent origin

10 0 10 20 30 40 50 feet
50 0 5 10 15 metres

3.11

erans in Gaul and England who presumably introduced skills they had learned in Italy.[20]

Texts by Roman agronomists such as Cato, Varro, Columella, Pliny, and Palladius were certainly preserved in monastic libraries. For example, Lorsch possessed a copy of Pliny, and Fulda had a Columella in the ninth century. Alcuin, the learned English monk in charge of Charlemagne's Palace School, would have been familiar with Pliny and many other writers whose works were in the library at York. But it is impossible to determine whether monks simply copied these texts or put them to practical use.[21]

The Romans introduced fruit cultivation to northern Gaul.[22] At St. Gall in Switzerland the orchard and kitchen garden of the abbey, described by Strabo, a monk who lived there during the first half of the ninth century, were laid out in the manner of a Roman *villa rustica*. At Corbie, in Picardy, there were similar extensive gardens.[23]

The estates underwent reorganization and better management between the eleventh and fourteenth centuries. A rapidly rising population resulted in extensive land clearances to increase food production. Yields of grain, although still low by modern and even some Roman standards, doubled between the Carolingian period and the thirteenth century. During the twelfth and thirteenth centuries rights to the ownership of tithes, which had been gradually appropriated by lay landlords, were returned to the abbeys and became a principal source of their wealth.[24] The spectacular tithe barns which remain attest to this.

In some areas, the cultivated fields around ancient Gallo-Roman villas were simply expanded.[25] In northern Germany and similar desolate regions, the Church and other magnates encouraged Dutch and Flemish colonists to drain and clear wastelands. Many of the new settlements were created by the landlords themselves, who supported the settlers initially with food, tools, and housing, and gave them favorable terms to remain.[26]

Increasingly monastic *demesnes* were leased out, either for cash rent or in return for up to half the harvest and the livestock raised on them. Distant estates were sold off or exchanged, and provisions needed by the monks were purchased instead from markets closer at hand. Eventually cash rents began to replace the foodstuffs and labor traditionally demanded from the peasants.

A major transformation in the exploitation of the estates occurred with the founding of the Cistercian order at the close of the eleventh century, which proved to be the greatest agricultural enterprise of the Middle Ages. Cîteaux was founded in Burgundy in 1098 in the belief that Cluny had become too worldly and had strayed from the basic principles of St. Benedict's Rule. It was followed in 1115 by Clairvaux.[27]

Whereas Cluny and the Benedictines relied on tenant farmers to fulfill their agricultural needs, the Cistercian monks transformed labor on their own lands into a form of devotion. By renouncing material wealth in favor of spiritual fulfillment they attracted the youthful elite of Europe and were donated vast landholdings. Although the ideals of the movement began to wane toward the close of the thirteenth century, by its end 742 monasteries had been established across Europe. Together they built an estimated ten to twenty thousand magnificent barns, among the finest ever raised.[28]

Intellectually gifted, the Cistercians were excellent administrators. Contrary to popular belief they did not settle in virgin, wilderness areas, although their initial reliance on pastoralism in forested regions may have given this impression. Indeed they were probably responsible for preserving extensive areas of forest, rather than denuding them, because they needed the woodland for their animals. Granted papal relief from payment of tithes in 1132, and exempted from tolls and other fees, they held a competitive advantage over their neighbors in selling such products as meat, hides, and wool from their animals at markets in the growing new towns.[29]

Because of their large herds and flocks they were better able to fertilize their fields, while others with few livestock had to resort to clearing marginal lands when their soils were exhausted. In southern France they used the profits from sheep, goats, pigs, and cattle to purchase land to add to properties already donated by local knights, who often entered the order themselves.

Eventually, when they had acquired more arable land than they could cultivate on their own, they invited peasants to join as lay brothers, or *conversi*. In return the peasants transferred hereditary rights to their holdings to the monasteries. Thus the Cistercians built up a skilled labor force which could be moved from grange to grange as the need arose, and because they owned the entire harvests produced on their lands, they needed huge barns to store them in.

As *conversi*, peasants were able to escape their irksome feudal obligations and reach for spiritual salvation. The stipulation that they remain celibate meant that the monasteries were not responsible for feeding unproductive family members. In the end, however, this was to prove a disadvantage because the labor force failed to replace itself.

In the fourteenth century the Bolognese writer Pietro de Crescenzi refocused attention on the work of the Roman agronomists. Whether the Cistercians anticipated him is impossible to tell, but their administration, architecture, and system of measurement certainly appear to bear the imprint of Rome.[30] They also constructed water mills for grinding grain, a technology introduced at the time of the Empire and improved upon in the thirteenth century with the introduction of the overshot wheel.[31]

The cultural renaissance that took place during Charlemagne's reign was repeated in the twelfth century. Church and political leaders renewed their study of classical texts, government, and art and architecture. Charlemagne himself undertook to erect the Palatine Chapel in Aachen "finer than the ancient buildings of the Romans [and] he summoned from all the lands beyond the seas architects and workmen skilled in every relevant art."[32] Latin, the universal language of the educated, enabled the elite to exchange fresh ideas, while the poor remained imprisoned within their regional dialects.

Like the Romans, the Benedictines and Cistercians dreaded fire and yearned for indestructible monuments. They replaced timber structures with others of masonry, and sheathed their barns with stone. The rebuilt abbey of Cluny was inspired by classical precedents. Henry of Blois, bishop of Winchester and a benefactor of Cluny, epitomized the prevailing attitude by traveling to Rome to purchase statuary.

Innovations in architecture and carpentry invariably occurred first in the monasteries, and later with the construction of the great Gothic cathedrals. Since both Cluny and the Cistercian movement were founded in Burgundy, its building traditions must have spread throughout Europe during the twelfth and thirteenth centuries. The plans for Fountains Abbey, for example, were carried to England from Clairvaux by Geoffrey d'Alaine, one of its monks and builders.[33]

These monasteries and their barns were constructed and repaired with the assistance of local builders, who imparted to each a regional character. But in return the demands made of the builders by the Church must have broadened their own knowledge and skills. By their very presence amongst rural communities, monks became catalysts for change throughout the Continent.

4.1: The seventh-century Saxon chapel of St. Peter-on-the-Wall at Bradwell in Essex, England, is built on the site of the Roman fort of Othona. Stripped of its Christian trappings, an apse and porticus, it bears a striking resemblance to a *horreum*.

Chapter 4
HORREUM, MONASTIC BARN

IN ROMAN ITALY cereals were usually harvested in June and July, and the threshing took place outdoors later in the season. Columella said that in the event of a sudden rain squall, crops being processed should be brought under shelter. Varro named the shelter a *nubilarium,* adding that it should be open on the side next to the threshing floor and should have windows for ventilation in the other.[1] He may well have been misinterpreted when he wrote this. If what he actually said was that the *nubilarium* had an *opening* on the side, like a door, then his description was of a side-entry barn similar to those excavated on other farms in Roman Italy.[2]

Vitruvius, an architect of the first century B.C., suggested to his readers that "*horrea* for grain, hay, and spelt . . . should be built apart from the farmhouse, so that farmhouses may be better protected against danger from fire." The storage of hay implies a building that functions at least partially as a barn. Fruits and wine might also have been kept within, along with tools and farm equipment. Indeed a third-century A.D. mosaic from Oudna in Tunisia illustrates a plow propped against the outside wall of one. Despite this, the *horreum* seems to have been regarded primarily as a granary, or *granarium,* for the two words were often used interchangeably. As a granary it sometimes had a vaulted ceiling.[3]

The *horreum* depicted in a villa scene from an early fifth-century mosaic found at Tabarka, Tunisia, is a monospan building with an entrance in one end and windows above, perhaps to ventilate an attic. This would conform with Columella's advice that "grain, hay, leaves, chaff and other fodder should be stored in lofts."[4]

On Trajan's Column, erected in Rome in 112 A.D. to commemorate the emperor's exploits against the Dacians (who occupied the region now known as Romania), are representations of several storehouses virtually interchangeable with the Tunisian example. Arrayed along the banks of the Danube, they are protected by timber palisades. Provisions brought by boat, including what appear to be casks of wine, are about to be unloaded into them.

Horrea were constructed by the Roman army throughout the Empire to hold grain and military equipment. The portrayal of identical storehouses as far apart as the Danube and North Africa suggests that comparable buildings were erected at forts and villas in Gaul and Britain also.

The seventh-century Saxon chapel at Bradwell in Essex stands at the entrance to a long-vanished Roman fort and is built of materials taken from the defensive wall. Stripped of its Christian trappings, an apse and porticus, it bears a striking resemblance to a *horreum*. So too did some Carolingian funerary shrines, and the two cell-like oratories within the cloister of the monastery of St. Riquier in Normandy, founded at the close of the eighth century.[5]

Because of the shorter growing season and damper climate of northern Europe, unthreshed grain had to be kept dry in a barn until it could be flailed over the winter (see color plate 5). Peasant women are shown carrying sheaves into such a *horreum* in a late twelfth-century manuscript from the middle Rhine. The scene is an allegorical one of the harvests women should expect to reap during their virginity, marriage, and widowhood. Another mid-thirteenth-century miniature from Paris illustrates a passage in Genesis in which Joseph filled the Egyptians' barns with grain during seven years of

4.2: An early fifth-century mosaic from Tabarka (known to the Romans as Thabraca) in Tunisia depicts the *villa urbana* of an affluent landowner, set in a garden with a pond and ducks in the foreground. A *horreum,* or granary, stands on the left corner of the villa.

4.3: *Horrea,* protected by stockades, line the banks of the Danube River in a scene from Trajan's Column. Casks of wine and sacks of grain or military equipment, transported here by boat, are about to be unloaded and stored within them. The column, erected in Rome in 112 A.D., commemorates Trajan's campaign against the Dacians, who occupied the region now known as Romania.

plenty and, during the seven years of famine that followed, opened the storehouses and sold the grain to them.[6] Comparable field barns still exist today in parts of Europe.

The fact that in Spain a granary is still referred to as a *hórreo* supports the premise that this monospan type has been in continuous use for almost two millennia. However, establishing precedents for the aisled *horreum* calls for a more circuitous approach.

The argument could be made that aisled monastic barns originated in the twelfth century, as a result of the restoration of tithes to the abbeys and the Cistercians' agricultural surpluses, which called for increased storage space on their granges. By adding aisles to the sides of a monospan *horreum,* the floor area could have been expanded by approximately two-thirds at considerably less cost than constructing

a new building. However, the precedents for aisled barns appear to extend even further back to the Roman period.

The oldest standing aisled barn in Europe, if the present structure is original, may well be one at Warnavillers, founded by the Cistercian abbey of Ourscamp in Picardy. It is mentioned in a document from 1150 A.D.[7] Others in France and England have been dated to the thirteenth century on estates once owned by orders such as the Benedictines, Templars, and Premonstratensians, as well as the Cistercians.

A deed of the abbey of Ourscamp, dated 1156, refers to *orreum grangie de Warnaviller* ("the barn within the grange of Warnavillers"), thereby distinguishing between the barn and the farm on which it stood.[8] In England, surviving twelfth-century lease agreements of

4.4: In this image taken from a Carolingian bookbinding in the collection of the Bibliothèque Nationale in Paris, the funerary chapel of Christ is depicted as a *horreum*.

4.6: This mid-thirteenth-century miniature from Paris illustrates the passage in Genesis in which Joseph filled the barns in Egypt following seven bountiful harvests.

4.5: In an allegorical scene from the *Jungfrauenspiegel*, an illuminated manuscript of the late twelfth century from the middle Rhine, widows store their harvest in a *horreum*, having reaped sixty times what they sowed. The married women below them reap only thirty times, while the blessed virgins above reap a hundredfold.

4.7: This ancient barn on the grange of Warnavillers (Oise) in Picardy originally belonged to the Cistercian abbey of Ourscamp. The first mention of a barn on the site is in 1150. The dove-cote in the foreground obstructs the view of a door in the southwest side which was inserted later. The original wagon door in the center of the southeast end has been blocked up.

4.8: The interior of the barn measures 111.5 feet by 62 feet (34 m by 19 m), and approximately 46 feet (14 m) to the ridge. Pairs of cylindrical stone piers 26 feet (8 m) high by 2.75 feet (0.8 m) in diameter carry triangular roof trusses, each made up of a tie-beam, a pair of rafters, and a vertical *poinçon,* or king post. The closely spaced coupled rafters are stiffened laterally by scissor braces.

4.10

4.9–4.10: The rafter feet are anchored to parallel arcade plates by means of short vertical ashlar pieces and horizontal sole pieces. The rafters spanning the nave do not end on the arcade plates, but extend down beyond them for a short distance. The carpenters employed a combination of mortise-and-tenon and lap joints, assembling the plates together atop the piers with *trait-de-Jupiter* scarf joints. (For further details of the roof construction see 8.1 and 8.2.)

4.9

St. Paul's Cathedral refer to the ecclesiastical barns as either *orrea* or *grangia*.[9]

The multifunctional nature of the Roman *horreum* has already been discussed. In addition to serving as a granary, it could be a storehouse for other agricultural produce, such as fruits and wine, and even a general warehouse. The *cella,* or *cellarium,* had a similar purpose. While it was usually regarded as a storage room for oil and wine, it could also be a larder for fruits, grain, and other foodstuffs.[10]

The early ninth-century *cellarium* of the monastery of Fontanella (St. Wandrille) in Normandy was adjacent to the refectory, separated from it by a masonry partition. At the nearby abbey of Jumièges (see color plate 6) there was a similar building, 290 feet long by 50 feet wide, with the monks' dormitory occupying the floor above. Clearly the cellars in these two instances acted as larders for a variety of foodstuffs.[11]

The *cellarium* came to be one of the three principal structures surrounding the medieval monastic cloister, usually located on the west side and communicating with the kitchen, bakery, and refectory. The Cistercian monastery of Clairvaux, founded in 1115 and motherhouse to the abbey of Ourscamp, had a two-story, three-aisled *cellarium et granaria majora* which survives to this day. It is believed to date to the mid-twelfth century, when the monastery was rebuilt farther down the valley from the original site. The fourteen-bay *granarium,* identical in plan to the *cellarium* immediately below it, is some 262.5 feet long by 58 feet wide (80 m by 17.7 m), and has octagonal stone arcade piers with a roof vaulted in the Roman manner.[12]

The *cellararius,* or cellarer, along with his subordinate the *custos panis,* or keeper of the bread, was responsible for provisioning the monastery, supervising the granges, and maintaining the outbuildings.[13] In 1384–85, the cellarer paid for repairs to the mangers on a farm belonging to Battle Abbey in England. A century later an entry in the cellarer's logbook at Durham records that he had "paid for building one barn at Rilley being called the wheatbarn."[14] St. Benedict of Nursia, the founder of Benedictine monasticism, referred to

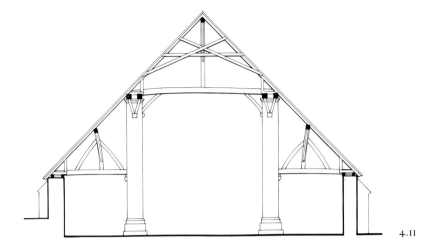

4.11

4.11, 4.12: A cross section, longitudinal section, and ground plan of the mid-twelfth-century barn at Warnavillers. The measurements are not completely reliable.

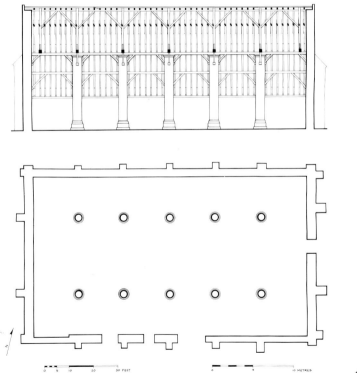

4.12

the position of *cellararius* in the sixth century, so it may have had a Roman origin.[15]

Clairvaux possessed two of the largest aisled *horrea* ever recorded. One, of an unprecedented seven aisles, believed to be 210 feet long by 120 feet wide (64 m by 36.5 m) and dating to the mid-twelfth century, was located at the *grangia Ultra Albam,* while another, of six aisles, stood on the site of the original abbey, the *monasterium vetus.* The latter had dwellings attached, along with a court and garden.[16] In both of these buildings the space was subdivided into aisles of equal breadth, while other barns nearby had unmistakable naves.

Near Saint-Aubin, at a site named "le Mazeret" (southeast of Dijon), the foundations of three large aisled buildings have been found within a Gallo-Roman villa complex. Two of the buildings measured about 165 feet by 100 feet (approximately 50 m by 30 m), and contained three aisles of equal width, while the third, smaller building nearby evidently had a nave, with porches on either side. The plans bear a striking resemblance to those of Clairvaux, although further excavation is clearly needed before any direct relationship can be established. Remains of similar buildings have been found on villas in Italy.[17]

If indeed the architecture of the monastic *cellarium* influenced that of the *horreum,* then the mid-eleventh-century cellar at Cluny merits attention. Even though Kenneth Conant's reconstruction of Cluny II (the second rebuilding of the monastery) is an unreliable guide, a visitor of the period did describe the *cellarium* as being 70 feet long by 60 feet broad, the same width as the one at Clairvaux. A three-aisled structure would almost certainly have been required to support a roof of this span. The storehouse left a lasting impression on another visitor, who made a note of it following a tour of the cloister around 1063.[18]

The most important architectural plan of the Carolingian era, drawn shortly after Charlemagne's death in 814 but never executed, was the Plan of St. Gall. In Walter Horn's words the Plan "owes its existence to the striving for a cultural unity. . . . [It was] the creation of an ideal scheme to standardize and guide monastic architecture for the future." One of the monastery's outbuildings contains the inscription *horreum et repositio fructuū annaliū* ("barn and storehouse for the annual grain harvest"). In its center is a cross-shaped area designated as "the place where grain and chaff are threshed."[19]

Horn interpreted this *horreum* as being aisled. Calculating its width to be 47.5 feet, he assumed that the roof of the barn must have been carried by two rows of freestanding posts, since 25 feet would have been about the maximum single span attainable at the time. If he is correct, then the three-aisled barn would have been familiar to monastic builders and planners throughout the Carolingian Empire in the ninth century, long before Cluny II was rebuilt. Moreover it leaves open the possibility that the barns on the royal villa at Annappes, surveyed around the time the Plan of St. Gall was drawn up, may also have been aisled (see page 42).[20]

References to *horrea* in Gaul are scarce between the end of the Roman period and the start of the Carolingian era. Gregory of Tours, describing the events of the sixth century, mentioned that the Frankish King Lothar I, son of Clovis, had been harshly criticized by Bishop Injuriosus for not feeding the poor from his own granaries. The storehouses and granaries of another wealthy individual had temporarily sustained defenders under siege in the town of Comminges. And in 590 A.D. came news that "the River Tiber had covered Rome with such flood-water that a number of ancient churches had collapsed and the papal granaries had been destroyed, with the loss of several thousand bushels of wheat."[21]

The remains of one papal *horreum* that survived have been excavated some fourteen kilometers from the center of Rome. It was a formidable building of basilican plan, measuring 259 feet by 62 feet (79 m by 19 m), built in the late fourth or early fifth century A.D. in an area previously occupied by modest, privately owned villas. One end probably contained residential quarters above a vaulted grain-storage chamber, to which was attached a substantial barn that had held agricultural produce or livestock. Since it was erected at a time when overseas grain supplies were shrinking, its size suggests that the Church had expropriated local properties for large-scale cereal production. It remained in use until late in the ninth century.[22]

By Late Antiquity the Church had assumed responsibility for food distribution in Rome, and this *horreum* may have become one of its chief supply depots. In Gaul others followed Rome's lead and fed the needy on a regular basis. In Burgundy a relative of Bishop Sidonius transported four thousand starving inhabitants to his villa and fed them from his own storehouses. St. Patiens, the bishop of Lyons, emulated his example.[23]

Not everyone, however, conducted himself in a manner befitting the Church's reputation. Notker, the stammering monk of St. Gall, wrote of a certain bishop "who was uncommonly parsimonious." Following a disastrous harvest in his district, "this miserly landlord, rejoicing in the ultimate necessity of all the inhabitants, who were already on the point of death, ordered his storehouses to be opened, so that supplies could be offered for sale at an exorbitant price."[24]

Evidently the monasteries in Gaul did possess granaries and barns, most probably ones they had taken over when the Romans left. In the former imperial capital of Trier a Benedictine convent, the "Monasterium S. Mariae vocatum Orrea" as it was known in 895, was discovered to have been built on the foundations of a pair of aisled fourth-century Roman *horrea*.[25]

Although they certainly were not commonplace, a number of aisled buildings have been excavated on villa sites in the provinces of Britain and Gaul. The Romano-British examples typically were farmhouses with living as well as storage space, and they appear to differ somewhat in proportion and function from Continental types.[26]

What is significant is that they were abandoned following the Roman withdrawal, and aisled construction in secular buildings ceased until reintroduced to England with the Norman Conquest. Current evidence suggests that none were built by the Saxon and Scandinavian invaders. Basilican churches, however, were erected during the Saxon period, all of which indicates that the influence stemmed ultimately from Rome itself.[27]

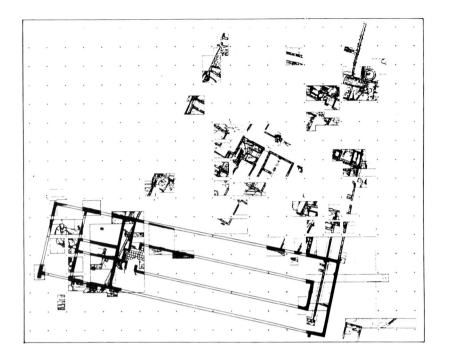

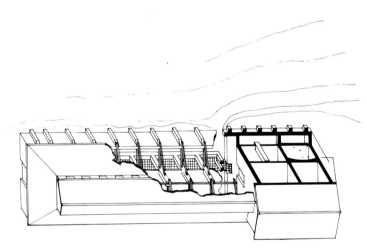

4.13: The ground plan and axonometric reconstruction of an aisled *horreum*, excavated on Via Gabina Site 10, just outside Rome, believed to have been built by the Church in the late fourth or early fifth century. It remained in use until the end of the ninth century. The overall dimensions are 259 feet by 62 feet (79 m by 19 m). Attached to the barn is a vaulted grain-storage chamber surmounted, perhaps, by residential quarters.

5.1

5.1–5.5: The Wehlburg farmhouse from Wehdel, north of Osnabrück in Lower Saxony, was built in 1750 and measures 118 feet by 46 feet (36 m by 14 m). It now stands on the grounds of the Cloppenburg open-air museum. The central wagon door (see detail in 7.4), with horse boxes just inside the deep entryway, leads directly onto the threshing floor. Only a prosperous farmer could afford such a handsomely decorated and jettied façade, which takes up one side of a courtyard bounded by other outbuildings. The gate in the right-hand corner leads through a garden to a doorway in the side of the living quarters at the far end.

62

Chapter 5
THE *HALLENHAUS*

DUTCH AND GERMAN settlers introduced a three-aisled farmhouse to North America which provided shelter for the family, livestock, and crops under the same roof. By the close of the seventeenth century it had been abandoned as a dwelling but continued in use as an aisled barn, the first on the American continent. Known in Germany as a *hallenhaus,* this building type still exists in the eastern provinces of the Netherlands and the northern German states of Lower Saxony, Westphalia, Schleswig-Holstein, and Mecklenburg. The *lös hoes,* a farmhouse with no partition dividing the living quarters from the barn, was common in the poorer districts of the Netherlands (see illustration 6.10).

Traditionally one end was taken up by the dwelling space, which was separated from the barn by the *flett,* an open area dominated by the hearth where the occupants gathered for warmth and light and to cook. From here the women, while spinning wool or flax, could observe the activity within the barn (see illustrations 6.9 and 6.11). The cattle stalled in the aisles faced in toward the nave, or *diele.* Wagon loads of unthreshed crops were trundled through large doors in the end onto the *diele,* which served as the threshing floor during the winter months.

Poles or planks were laid across the beams that spanned the nave, creating a loft into which the harvest was pitched. Hay and surplus cereals were stored outside, either in unaisled barns or in stacks often protected by adjustable roofs (*rutenbergs*).[1] Smoke curling up to the rafters not only cured the meat suspended above the hearth but also served to drive insects from the grain kept in the attic. Contrary to popular belief, the harvest was too densely packed to be dried by heat from the fire.

The *hallenhaus* rarely stood alone except in the humblest circumstances. One of the earliest outbuildings was the granary, or *speicher,* located within sight of the farmhouse. Here seed grain was kept to prevent it from being damaged by smoke within the farmhouse, as well as to serve the immediate needs for baking bread. The *speicher* was daubed with clay or faced with brick as protection against fire and sometimes surrounded by a defensive moat.[2] Ancillary buildings might include a bakehouse, cart shed, pigsty, and a sheepfold where valuable sheep manure accumulated.

Three-aisled buildings existed in northern Europe as early as 1700 B.C., almost two millennia before the Roman occupation of Gaul, along the plain stretching from the Netherlands to southern Denmark.[3] In the region of Bremerhaven in Lower Saxony, Germany, excavations have revealed the middle Bronze Age ancestor of the *hallenhaus* to be a narrow, open-sided shed averaging 80 to 90 feet in length, but up to 230 feet (70 m) in exceptional cases. Its size suggests it was occupied by an extended family.

Essentially it was a roof without walls. The low walls were constructed separately of sods, replaced later by wattle daubed with clay, and since they were freestanding they carried no load. The roof consisted of closely spaced pairs of rafters, each pair supported by four posts set in the ground for stability, two in the planes of the outer walls, and the other two nearer the middle of the house. The four parallel rows of posts thus created a narrow central nave flanked by aisles.[4]

The nearby remains of unaisled barns, granaries, or storage pits indicate that crops were kept outside the main building. The houses became smaller during the late Bronze Age, perhaps because they

5.2

5.3

5.4

5.5

5.6: The *diele,* or threshing floor, viewed from the wagon entry, is flanked by stalls for the livestock. Planks laid across thé beams form the floor of the loft above (see detail in 8.20). The door in the partition at the far end of the nave, which divides the barn from the dwelling, leads to an open living area (the *flett*) containing a hearth for cooking.

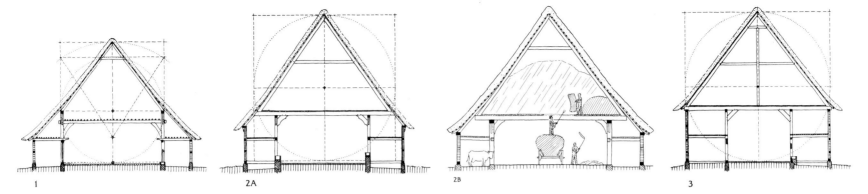

5.7: Examples of three different methods employed in farmhouses to increase the storage space above the nave:

1) Anchor-beams effectively lower the loft floor in the eastern Netherlands and adjacent region of Germany.

2A) To the east and south the tie-beams, or *dachbalken,* are cantilevered over the tops of the arcade posts to create a *zweiständerhaus,* or two-post house.

2B) In this cross section of a *zweiständerhaus* a wagon stands on the *diele,* or threshing floor, as the harvest is pitched up into the attic. The cattle face the interior of the barn..

3) In the *vierständerhaus,* or four-post house, the posts in the outer walls are the same height as the arcade posts and the *dachbalken* continue all the way across the building to meet them.

were now occupied by individual families with fewer cattle. Evidence that an elite class had emerged in this tribal society by the early Iron Age comes from scattered burial sites containing prestigious possessions.[5]

Entries on either side of the typical farmhouse led into a cross-passage dividing the living quarters, centered around an open hearth, from the byre occupying the other half. The cows were taken to their stalls through an opening in the end. In some settlements the actual hoofprints of livestock have been uncovered.[6] Unlike in the medieval *hallenhaus,* these buildings had the cows' rumps facing inward so that precious manure could be collected in trenches lined with wattle mats in the nave. As much as three-quarters of the herd had to be slaughtered every autumn for lack of winter fodder.[7] By comparing the stall sizes, archaeologists have deduced that cattle became smaller between the Bronze Age and medieval times.[8]

Settlements in the more fertile, marshy coastal district now known as Frisia were built upon elevated mounds (*terpen* in Dutch) of dung and local clay. The people living farther inland on sandy islands surrounded by bogs (known as *geest*) had access to better timber supplies, and as a result their farmhouses were distinctly sturdier. Buildings in the clay and sandy districts remained essentially similar until about 600 A.D., but after the third century A.D. the inland ones began to lengthen again as extra work space and possibly storage for barley and oats were added. Rye, which had been considered a weed up until the first century, became increasingly important in the diet and was kept in pits outside. Hay, because of the danger of spontaneous combustion, presumably was also left outdoors in stacks.

By the late fifth century, farmhouses in the *geest* region had once more reached 130 feet to 200 feet (40 m to 60 m) in length, a reflection perhaps of greater harvests and an increasing number of activities taking place under the one roof. Fertilizer was now being collected in sunken cattle stalls partially filled with sods from the moors, which, when mixed with dung, formed a rich turf manure, or *plaggen*.[9] These long farmhouses were succeeded by shorter ones surrounded by separate granaries and huts, in which items such as millstones were made for trade with communities on the *terpen*.

5.8, 5.9: The window alcove in the Haakenhof farmhouse at Cloppenburg contains a dining table and chairs. The *flett* has a patterned floor of pebbles and flagstones. The short passageway to the right leads to the entranceway in the side of the house. Doors to the left lead to sleeping quarters at the end of the dwelling section.

5.8

5.9

5.10: A view from the *flett* of the Wehlburg house showing, on the right, the other side of the partition with its doorway leading into the *diele*. Under the windows to the left is the dining niche. Between the two is a second doorway leading to the exterior. Meat hung from racks above the fire was cured by the smoke.

5.11: Beyond the *flett* of the Wehlburg house is the *stube*, a living room heated by a stove and lined with cupboard-beds.

5.12

5.12, 5.13: In modest homes, bed alcoves were located near the hearth, partly for warmth and partly to enable the inhabitants to keep watch over the fire at night. The cooking pot hanging from the wood crane over the flames could be conveniently swung away from the heat. The coals were kept in place with an iron fireguard. These interior views are of the Saterhaus and Müllerhaus, respectively, at the Cloppenburg open-air museum in Lower Saxony, Germany.

5.13

5.14: A fine *hallenhaus* from Grönloh in Lower Saxony, built in 1764. The high sidewalls are typical of a farmhouse of *vierständer* (four-post) construction (see 5.7, number 3).

5.15: The remains of an aisled cattle byre of the second century B.C., elevated above sea level on a raised mound, were excavated in the 1930s by A. E. van Giffen at Ezinge (Groningen) in the Netherlands. The building, measuring over 75 feet (23 m) long and 29 feet (7.2 m) wide, had entries at each end for the livestock. The narrow nave is flanked by woven mats for the collection of manure. The cattle were stalled, face outward, in wattle partitions on either side. Stubs of the oak posts that supported the roof are clearly visible.

Over time attempts were made to widen the constricting nave by spacing the inner posts increasingly farther apart, until eventually they merged with the outer wall posts. Innovations in construction invariably originated in the Netherlands, taking a century to spread to the coastal areas of Lower Saxony, and a further century to reach Jutland in Denmark.[10] By the fifth century part of the living area of farmhouses in the Drenthe region in the northeastern Netherlands had already become an open space.[11]

A great migration of Germanic people took place between the fifth and early seventh centuries, as Saxons and other tribes scattered across a wide area abandoned their homelands to settle in England. The buildings erected there by the Anglo-Saxons were much shorter, resembling the unaisled section of the Netherlands farmhouse. Since no byres have been found in them, the implication is that either the soil was better suited to growing crops than cattle raising, or that the animals were wintered outdoors because of the warmer climate. The appearance of ancillary buildings, including sunken huts in which cloth was possibly woven, points to the decentralization of craft production.[12]

Around 630 A.D., toward the end of the Migration Period, sizable settlements like the one at Dalem reappeared unexpectedly in northern Germany. These buildings were also unaisled, their interiors unobstructed by posts, and cattle were stalled within freestanding wattle partitions. Then, commencing in the ninth century, lean-tos, or *outshots,* were gradually added to portions of one or both of the exterior walls.

Developments during the twelfth to fourteenth centuries are a mystery. Virtually no traces of buildings remain. It is ironic that having been able to follow the evolution of the farmhouse from the Bronze Age through to the eleventh/twelfth century, archaeologists should understand so little about the changes that occurred from then on to the fifteenth century. The explanation lies in a dramatic improvement in construction.

Before the eleventh/twelfth century, houses were built with earth-fast posts, or timbers sunk into holes in the ground. The dampness in the soil caused them to rot fairly rapidly, with the result that buildings had to be replaced every twenty-five years or so. Their remains show up in the form of dark blotches on the lighter-colored soil, enabling archaeologists to plot the positions, diameters, depths, and angles of the posts. Although they clearly show the layout of a farmhouse, attempts to reconstruct the frame and roof are based on educated guesswork.

The twelfth to early fourteenth centuries mark the transition from vulnerable earthfast posts to timbers set off the ground on stone pads. These were boulders taken from glacial moraines, and because they were scarce they were transported to a new site whenever a building was abandoned. It is precisely this improvement which has frustrated archaeologists. Having no postholes to guide them, they can only speculate on evolutionary developments by working backward from the construction of the earliest standing houses.[13]

The farmhouse that reemerges in the fifteenth century is the three-aisled *hallenhaus,* sheltering the family and its livestock and crops under one roof. At some point prior to this, perhaps in the twelfth/thirteenth century, the outshots must have been converted into sunken cattle stalls. The livestock were turned to face the interior of the single-span house, which now became a wide nave and assumed the function of a barn with crop storage in the loft.

Functionally the *hallenhaus* differs from its predecessors in that, while they may have had some space for crop storage, they were essentially shelters for people and livestock. The naves were narrow passageways for the collection of manure rather than for threshing, and cattle faced the outer walls.

It also differs structurally in that it is a freestanding, single-span building with lean-tos added to the sides to create aisles (see illustrations 6.4 to 6.8). The arcade posts carry the full load of the roof. The outshots are simply an adjunct with secondary rafters extending from the feet of the main rafters across the aisle to the horizontal *plate* atop the outer wall posts.[14] The collapse of an aisle would not affect the building as a whole, as it would in Bronze and Iron Age houses. In this respect, the *hallenhaus* resembles the monastic barn, which leads to an examination of possible links between the two buildings.

Chapter 6

AISLED BARNS IN NORTH AMERICA

COLONEL PHILIP SCHUYLER, commander of the American forces opposing the British in the battle at Saratoga, owned a substantial barn north of Albany, New York. Toward the end of the eighteenth century, just prior to the Revolutionary War, he was visited by Anne Grant, who upon her return home to Scotland recalled the experience in her memoirs.

Adjoining to the orchard was the most spacious barn I ever beheld; which I shall describe for the benefit of such of my readers as have never seen a building constructed on a plan so comprehensive. This barn . . . was of a vast size, at least an hundred feet long, and sixty wide. The roof rose to a very great height in the midst, and sloped down till it came within ten feet of the ground, when the walls commenced; which, like the whole of this fabric, was formed of wood. It was raised three feet from the ground, by beams resting on stone; and on these beams were laid in the middle of the building a very massive oak floor. Before the door was a large sill, sloping downwards, of the same materials. About twelve feet in breadth on each side of this capacious building were divided off for cattle; on one side ran a manger, at the above mentioned distance from the wall, the whole length of the building, with a rack above it; on the others were stalls for other cattle, running also the whole length of the building. The cattle and horses stood with their hinder parts to the wall, and their heads projecting towards the threshing floor. There was a prodigious large box or open chest in one side built up, for holding the corn after it was thrashed; and the roof, which

was very lofty and spacious, was supported by large cross beams; from one to the other of these was stretched a great number of long poles, so as to form a sort of open loft, on which the whole rich crop was laid up. The floor of those parts of the barn, which answered the purposes of a stable and cow-house, was made of thick slab deals, laid loosely over the supporting beams. And the mode of cleaning those places was by turning the boards, and permitting the dung and litter to fall into the receptacles left open below for the purpose: from thence, in spring they were often driven down the river, the soil in its original state not requiring the aid of manure. In the front of this vast edifice there were prodigious folding doors, and two others that opened behind.

Certainly never did cheerful rural toils wear a more exhilarating aspect than while the domestics were lodging the luxuriant harvest in this capacious repository. When speaking of the doors, I should have mentioned that they were made in the gable ends; those in the back equally large, to correspond with those in the front; while on each side of the great doors were smaller ones, for the cattle and horses to enter. Whenever the corn or hay was reaped or cut, and ready for carrying home, which in that dry and warm climate happened in a very few days, a wagon loaded with hay, for instance, was driven into the midst of this great barn, loaded also with numberless large grasshoppers, butterflies, and cicadas, who came along with the hay. From the top of the wagon, this was immediately forked up into the loft of the barn, in the midst of which was an open space left for the purpose; and then the unloaded

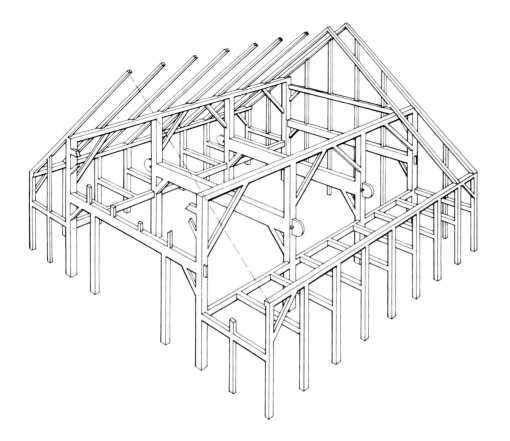

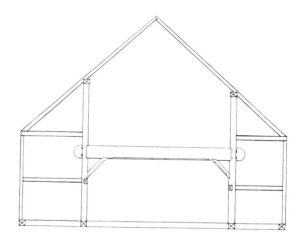

6.1: (*Left*) A cutaway perspective of the Dutch-built barn that once stood at Mickel Hollow, near Cobleskill (Schoharie County), New York. Not shown are the sill beams under the posts in the nave and outer walls, or the plank threshing floor (see 6.4 and 6.5). Typically such barns have an almost square floor plan. (*Right*) A section of the middle bent of the larger Bradt barn, near Fonda, New York, which had aisles of unequal width (see also 2.5) and a chamfered anchor-beam 12 inches by 24 inches (30.5 cm by 61 cm) in cross section. The building was destroyed by fire.

wagon drove, in rustic state, out of the great door at the other end. In the meantime every member of the family witnessed, or assisted in this summary process; by which the building and thatching of stacks was at once saved; and the whole crop and cattle were thus compendiously lodged under one roof.

The cheerfulness of this animated scene was much heightened by the quick appearance, and vanishing of the swallows; who twittered among their high-built dwellings in the roof. Here, as in every other instance, the safety of these domestic friends was attended to; and an abode provided for them. In the front of this barn were many holes, like those of a

pigeon-house, for the accommodation of the martin: that being the species to which this kind of home seems most congenial; and, in the inside of the barn, I have counted above fourscore at once. In the winter, when the earth was buried deep in new fallen snow, and no path fit for walking in was left, this barn was like a great gallery, well suited for that purpose; and furnished with pictures, not unpleasing to a simple and contented mind. As you walked through this long area, looking up, you beheld the abundance of the year treasured above you; on one side the comely heads of your snorting steeds presented themselves arranged in seemly order; on the other, your kine displayed their meeker visages, while the perspective on either, was terminated by heifers and fillies no less interesting. In the midst, your servants exercised the flail; and even, while they threshed out the straw, distributed it to the expectants on both sides; while the "liberal handful" was occasionally thrown to the many colored poultry on the sill. Winter itself never made this abode of life and plenty cold and cheerless. Here you might walk and view all your subjects, and their means of support, at one glance; except, indeed, the sheep, for whom a large and commodious building was erected very near the barn: the roof of which was furnished with a loft large enough to contain hay sufficient for their winter's food.

Col. Schuyler's barn was by far the largest I have ever seen: but all of them, in that country, were constructed on the same plan, furnished with the same accommodation, and presented the same cheering aspect.[1]

Schuyler himself was of Dutch extraction, and the aisled barn so vividly described by Mrs. Grant developed from the *hallenhaus*, which was introduced to North America by Dutch and German settlers early in the seventeenth century. New Netherland, a colony founded by the Dutch West India Company and centered along New York's Hudson River Valley, remained under Dutch control from 1614 to 1664 before it was eventually ceded to the British. Almost half of the settlers, farmers, soldiers, carpenters, and other craftsmen came from outside the Netherlands itself, including areas of present-day Germany, Belgium, and France.[2]

Presumably their first houses were attempts to replicate the traditional architecture of their homelands. None survives today, but there is documentary evidence that the settlers did build a *hallenhaus* similar if not identical to the Old World version. Quite likely a carpenter versed in one tradition erected a house for a client familiar with another, resulting in a hybrid building.

In 1642 Willem Kieft, the director of New Netherland, contracted with the carpenter Jeuriaen Hendricksen for a farmhouse to be erected on Manhattan island, New York.[3] It was to be 100 feet long by 24 feet wide, divided equally into barn and dwelling. The agreement stipulated that the rafters of the barn section were to be extended to create *uytlaeten* (outshots, or aisles) on either side, 9 and 10 feet in width, giving it an overall dimension of 50 feet by 43 feet.[4] This confirms the findings of European archaeologists that the *hallenhaus* evolved from an unaisled structure, to which lean-tos were subsequently added.

The almost-square ground plan of Kieft's barn resembles that of barns still standing in New York State, although the rafters of later examples are of one piece rather than interrupted at the arcade posts. This is probably because of the availability of tall, straight pines in the New World. The roof may well have been thatched. In the same year, David Pietersen de Vries noted that a fellow Dutchman had been shot dead while thatching his barn.[5]

Little is known of Kieft's background, but as director of New Netherland he surely decided what type of house he wanted. His carpenter came from Osenbrugge (Osnabrück in Lower Saxony), where the familiar farmhouse was a *hallenhaus*. One wonders whether Kieft chose a builder able to reproduce a house he felt comfortable with or whether Hendricksen was selected because no other carpenter was available at the time.

With only a limited number of craftsmen, similar situations must have occurred throughout the colony. What finally emerged on the family farm was a three-aisled barn similar to those that today stand in the Achterhoek area, along the Dutch-German border, although certain constructional features are decidedly different. In America this type of barn has come to be known as a "Dutch barn," which is a rather misleading term, given the remarkable diversity of barns in the Netherlands itself.[6]

Around 1643 a French Jesuit priest named Isaac Jogues was taken prisoner by Mohawk Indians while proselytizing west of Albany, New York. One account mentions that "he and his Indian masters were lodged together in a large building, like a barn, belonging to a Dutch farmer. It was 100 feet long, and had no partition of any kind.

6.2: Stripped of weatherboards to expose its 60-foot-by-50-foot (18.25 m by 15.25 m) timber frame, the late eighteenth-century Deertz barn stands here at its original location in Middleburgh (Schoharie County), New York, prior to being dismantled and moved.

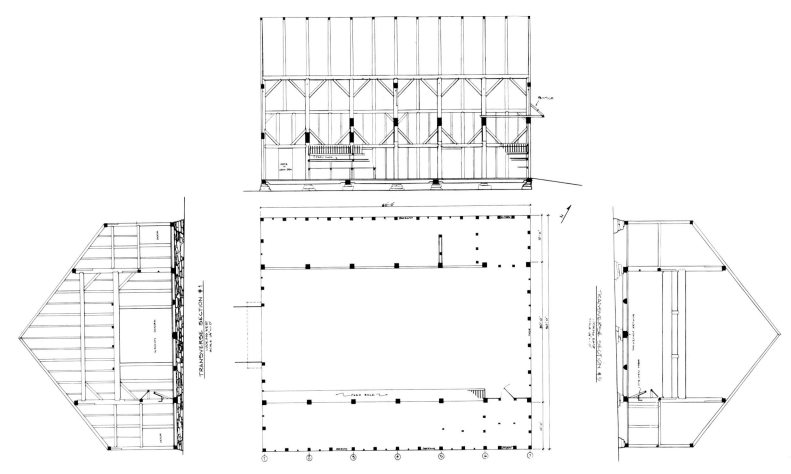

6.3: Sections of the Deertz barn. Since the roof is carried by the arcade posts, the collapse of a wall would not cause the entire structure to cave in. The posts do not rest on pad stones as in Europe, but are tenoned instead into longitudinal timber sills.

At one end the farmer kept his cattle; at the other he slept with his wife, a Mohawk squaw, and his children, while his Indian guests lay on the floor in the middle."[7]

If it were possible to verify the story, this would indeed be proof that the undivided *lös hoes* had made the transition to America. However, another biography of Jogues gives a conflicting version:

The owner was a Dutch farmer, a man of some substance and influence. He was married to a Mohawk woman and had several children by her. The structure in which he lived was a frame building about one hundred feet long. On one end of it was his home, solidly built and consisting of several rooms. A back door opened from the house into the barn. Here the

6.4

6.4–6.8: The reerection of the six-bay Deertz barn on a new site in Columbia County, New York, retraces the steps by which its ancestor, the *hallenhaus,* evolved from a monospan building to an aisled one with the subsequent addition of outshots. First the seven transverse frames or bents (from the Dutch word *gebint*), which make up the core of the building, are raised into position (6.4). The posts and anchor-beams (see detail in 6.7) together enclose the nave with its threshing floor of thick hemlock planks (6.5). Next the aisles are attached to either side. In the *hallenhaus* separate oak rafters span the nave and aisle respectively (see 5.7 numbers 1 and 2), whereas in North America rafters of pine sweep unbroken from ridge to eave (6.6 and 6.8).

6.5

6.6

6.7

6.8

6.9–6.11: This Dutch *lös hoes* from Zeijen in Drenthe, with the barn to the left and living quarters on the right, now stands on the grounds of the open-air museum at Arnhem. Similar farmhouses may have been built in the American colony of New Netherland during the seventeenth century. The packed earth threshing floor is flanked by sunken cattle stalls. Poles laid across the anchor-beams form a floor for the storage loft above. The *diele* leads onto the pebbled floor of the *flett*. Here smoke from the open fire cured meat and sausage suspended from racks above. Women brought in additional income by weaving cloth on looms like the one just visible in the room to the left.

6.10

6.11

party of savages slept. Beyond, at the far end, were the stalls of the horses and the cattle. A picket fence extended around the farmyard and building.[8]

Given the length of the farmhouse and the prosperity of its owner, the second description is likely to be the more accurate one.

The experience of Jasper Danckaerts, an agent for a Calvinist sect intent on founding a colony in America, provides one plausible explanation why settlers abandoned the *hallenhaus* in favor of a separate farmhouse and barn. In 1679, while scouting for suitable property, he spent a fitful night as guest of the farmer Jacques Cortelyou in New Utrecht (present-day Brooklyn, New York).

After supper [he wrote in his journal], we went to sleep in the barn, upon some straw spread with sheep-skins, in the midst of the continual grunting of hogs, squealing of pigs, bleating and coughing of sheep, barking of dogs, crowing of cocks, cackling

of hens, and, especially, a good quantity of fleas and vermin, of no small portion of which we were participants; and all with an open barn door, through which a northwest wind was blowing.[9]

No doubt another consideration was the severity of the North American winter, when the traditional earthen floor would have been unbearably frigid. Arguments have frequently been raised that heat from the livestock, combined with a fire in the hearth and deep layers of insulating straw in the loft, must have kept the occupants relatively snug. But tests in Germany have dispelled this myth. Indoor temperatures hovered a mere 4° to 6° C higher than those outside, and farm families were constantly afflicted with rheumatism.[10] During the hot and humid summers, flies and mosquitoes would have been an additional irritant.

In the Old World, cattle were housed in sunken stalls filled with a bedding of heather sods. The resulting turf manure, or *plaggen*, had a

83

6.12: The south gable of the Teller-Schermerhorn barn, which once stood near Schenectady, New York, had the low sidewalls and same steep roof profile as its counterparts from the Old World. It too has been destroyed.

rather sweet smell, or so it is claimed. As the need for *plaggen* diminished with the advent of artificial fertilizers in the nineteenth century, straw was substituted as litter instead. This resulted in a pungent odor which, because of poor ventilation, may have led to the introduction of partitions between dwelling space and barn in formerly undivided farmhouses.[11] Since no heaths existed in New Netherland, families may have avoided the stench by segregating their houses and barns.

One of the earliest references to a separate barn was in March of 1682, when Cornelius van Dyck agreed to lease his land at Catskill, New York, to Andries and Hendrick Jansen on the condition that "as rental of the said land [they] shall deliver a proper dwelling house . . . likewise a barn of fifty-two and a half feet long and as wide as the barn Marte Gerritse has built there."[12]

A few years earlier, in 1675, Harmen Bastiaensen had agreed to build a four-bay barn for Jan Maertensen in Kinderhook, New York. It was to be 50 feet long by 26 feet wide, with outshots, or *uytlaeten*, 10 feet deep on either side, one of which was to contain a horse manger for 40 feet of its length. The double door in one end, sufficiently generous for wagons to enter the threshing floor, was to be flanked by smaller doors allowing the livestock to enter the aisles directly. The roof detail, "at each end a gable with a sloping peak," suggests the hipped, or *wolfdak,* roof sometimes found in the Netherlands farmhouse (see illustration 6.10).[13]

Such roofs are common in the windy coastal areas of Germany and the Netherlands, implying that one of their functions is for longitudi-

6.13: This eighteenth-century barn from the "De Haimer" farm at Twekkelo, near Enschede in the Netherlands, was once used clandestinely by Mennonites as a church.

nal support. In Kent, England, the roofs of a number of fifteenth- and sixteenth-century barns are hipped at one end and gabled at the other. The hips have no additional reinforcement, but the rafters at the gabled terminals are braced against the wind, indicating the carpenters' concern that the roof might overturn without them.[14] Late aisled barns in the New World have gabled roofs, like those in the Achterhoek region of the Netherlands.

Peter Kalm was a naturalist who was commissioned by the Swedish Academy of Sciences to carry out botanical research in the American colonies. From September 1748 to February 1751 he journeyed through Pennsylvania, New Jersey, New York, and southern Canada, keeping a meticulous journal of his travels. If any *hallenhaus* still existed he surely would have recorded it. As it was, he was sufficiently impressed by the barns he saw en route from Trenton to New Brunswick to make this comment:

The barns had a peculiar kind of construction in this locality, of which I shall give a concise description. The main building was very large almost the size of a small church; the roof was high, covered with wooden shingles, sloping on both sides, but not steep. The walls which supported it were not much higher than a full grown man; but on the other hand the breadth of the building was all the greater. In the middle was the threshing floor and above it, or in the loft or garret, they put the unthrashed grain, the straw, or anything else, according to the season. On one side were stables for the

6.14: A five-bay barn of anchor-beam construction from Vreden-Ellewick in Westphalia, Germany, built around 1775 and now moved to the Westphalian open-air museum at Detmold. Its jettied gable resembles that of the Verplanck–Van Wyck barn in New York's Hudson Valley. Other than stabling an occasional horse or sheep, the building was used chiefly for the storage of hay or straw.

horses, and on the other for the cows. The young stock had also their particular stables or stalls, and in both ends of the building were large doors, so that one could drive in with a cart and horses through one of them, and go out at the other. Here under one roof therefore were the thrashing floor, the barn, the stables, the hay loft, the coach house etc. This kind of building is used chiefly by the Dutch and Germans, for it is to be observed that the country between Trenton and New York is not inhabited by many Englishmen, but mostly by Germans or Dutch, the latter of which are especially numerous.[15]

The use of wattle and daub for the walls of houses in the Netherlands left them vulnerable to the rain. Consequently the roofs swept low to the ground as Kalm noted, sheltering the sides under deep eaves. Such precautions should have been unnecessary in the New World, where there were ample timber supplies for weatherboarding. Nevertheless, it is clear settlers still clung to Old World customs as late as the mid-eighteenth century. It is quite conceivable that barns of the late seventeenth century had doors at opposite ends, allowing the wagons a through passage, but Kalm's is the first confirmation of such a feature.

Monospan barns have been excavated on middle Bronze Age sites in the Netherlands, but the three-aisled barn seems to be a late development there. Used for the storage of surplus crops rather than for animals, it materialized in the Twente district in the early eighteenth century.[16] Although the appearance of a separate aisled barn in America coincides roughly with its manifestation in Twente, the fact that livestock were stalled in the aisles of the New World barn, as they had been in the *hallenhaus,* seems to point to its independent evolution in North America.

Farmers do not give up long-standing traditions readily, but the settlers presumably were obliged to alter their dwellings in response to an unfamiliar climate, soils, and building materials, just as their Saxon forebears did when they migrated to England in the fifth century A.D. The process may have been accelerated when they came under British rule in 1664.

Although the aisled barn outlived its usefulness in the Hudson Valley during the nineteenth century, it did not disappear. Since its first introduction on the Atlantic seaboard in the late seventeenth century, it has spread across the North American continent to the shores of the Pacific, a tribute to its remarkable adaptability.[17]

7.1: A late eighteenth-century farmhouse at Köhlen, near Bremerhaven in Lower Saxony.

Chapter 7

DIFFUSION OR INDEPENDENT EVOLUTION?

THE SUGGESTION that monasteries may have had some influence on the development of the *hallenhaus* is bound to meet with a degree of skepticism, given the current paucity of documentary and archaeological evidence. Nevertheless several German and Dutch scholars suspect this is exactly what happened, without being able to specify precisely how.[1] The Church established a secure foothold in northern Germany only with the subjugation of the Saxons by Charlemagne in 803 A.D., although missionaries had begun preaching in the region the previous century.

The archaeologist Haio Zimmermann discovered a ninth-century structure in Lower Saxony which, judging by its exceptional timbers, almost 18 inches (45 cm) in diameter, must have belonged to an individual or institution of considerable importance. It was unaisled like neighboring buildings, but far more impressive in scale, measuring 120 feet by 33 feet (37 m by 10 m). Sometime later narrow outshots were attached halfway along either side, extending its overall width to 43 feet (13 m).[2] The fact that it was larger than any wooden church constructed in the region up to 1000 A.D. led Zimmermann to believe it may have been a *zehntscheune*, or tithe barn, but he confesses there is no further evidence to substantiate this claim.

To the west, in the Netherlands, the ground plan of the eleventh-century three-aisled timber church of St. Walburg matched those of local barns. There are differing opinions as to whether such houses of worship were simply consecrated farm buildings, or whether the Church itself was responsible for the introduction of aisled construction.[3]

Southwest of the lower Rhine, not far from the *hallenhaus* hearth region, a team of Dutch archaeologists has been excavating settlements in an area bounded by the Meuse, Demer, and Scheldt rivers. The district was occupied by native tribes during the Roman occupation, gradually abandoned during the third century, then reoccupied by Franks from across the Rhine, beginning in the mid-fourth century.[4]

When Anglo-Saxon missionaries led by Willibrord arrived here at the close of the seventh century, they were welcomed by the Frankish nobility, who, in a bid for salvation, began donating parts of their estates to the Church. Colonists cleared these tracts of forest during the first half of the eighth century, and the monasteries then converted them into manorial complexes.

This transformation coincided with a totally different building tradition, which emerged around 750 A.D. The earlier scattered farmhouses of the Merovingian era had been two-aisled, that is to say, with a line of ridgeposts supporting the roof along its longitudinal axis. They were replaced by sturdier three-aisled houses which were double the size of the former buildings. Their greater dimensions may reflect the need for extra storage space to hold the crops, although one would assume that surplus produce would have been taken to barns belonging to the manor itself.[5]

It has been argued that since the land clearances were instigated by stewards acting on behalf of the Church, the monasteries themselves were probably responsible for the introduction of this new Carolingian farmhouse, which, unlike the *hallenhaus*, incorporated aisles as an integral part of the structure.[6]

On the other hand, the transformation of the landscape resulted in a dramatic change in the agricultural economy. The animals best adapted to forage in woodlands were pigs, but with the opening up

7.2: *Landscape with Farmhouse,* a painting by the Dutch artist Cornelis van Dalem (c. 1535–1573), depicts an aisled peasant farmhouse in front of a ruined Gothic abbey, or conceivably the remains of a monastic barn with an attached watchtower (see 7.3). Centuries earlier the land was cleared by ancestors of these peasants, encouraged by the Church to settle here as colonists.

of pastures the emphasis changed to cattle raising.

Cattle were kept within the farmhouse itself because they constituted the medieval peasant family's most valuable asset. It is no coincidence that the name stems from the Latin *capitale,* and hence the derivation of the term *chattel*. The advantage of a three-aisled building was that it permitted livestock to be stalled in the aisles, while the nave could serve as a feeding passage.[7] However, aisles were not a prerequisite. Indeed the immediate precursor of the *hallenhaus* was a monospan building in which livestock were presumably penned behind wattle hurdles, and in a number of other regions the open longhouse seemed perfectly adequate.

Besides the *hallenhaus,* aisled multipurpose buildings were constructed throughout Europe during the Middle Ages. The Höfstetten, which once stood near Nürnberg, had a square ground plan with aisles on all four sides. It was built in 1367–68, a century earlier than the oldest known *hallenhaus*. A watercolor of the village of Kalchreuth by Albrecht Dürer depicts farmhouses very similar to it which remained in use until the nineteenth century, a tribute to their remarkable versatility. The Bauhofscheune, built not far away at Windsheim around 1441, is an aisled municipal granary with a roof of churchlike complexity, and similar examples may also have existed in Italy at this time.[8] Excavations conducted in 1992, as yet unpublished,

7.3: The thirteenth-century barn of the Cistercian abbey of Maubuisson (Val-d'Oise) in France measured 78 feet by 33 feet (24 m by 10 m) before the east aisle was demolished in the nineteenth century. The longitudinal section of the barn with its watchtower bears a distinct resemblance to the ruined building in the painting by Cornelis van Dalem (see 7.2).

suggest that there were aisled houses in the region of Regensburg, Bavaria, during the eighth or ninth centuries.[9]

If the barn represented in the Plan of St. Gall was aisled, as Walter Horn interpreted it to be, then such barns should have been present on monastic estates during the Carolingian period and probably earlier. Some of the first granges built by the Cistercians in the twelfth century housed lay brothers, livestock, crops, and farm equipment under a single roof.[10] Aisled barns and farmhouses may be found today throughout France, from Aquitaine to Champagne, as well as in the Jura region of Switzerland and in the Spanish Pyrenees.[11] Writing during the nineteenth century, Viollet-le-Duc

described how cattle were stalled in a barn adjacent to the church of St.-Martin-au-Bois, in the *département* of Oise, France, which had a large storage space above for forage.[12]

While they are similar in some respects to buildings in the eastern Netherlands and northern Germany, it is difficult to fathom how they might be related. Archaeologists might argue that they evolved independently of one another and that such resemblances are bound to occur when there are only a limited number of ways to accommodate farmers' requirements.

On the other hand, it is conceivable they were a product of colonization and land clearance. As in eighteenth-century America, the

7.4

7.4, 7.5: The arched wagon door of the mid-eighteenth-century Wehlburg house (see 5.1) shows the influence of ecclesiastic stone architecture, such as the door to the thirteenth-century monastic barn at Parçay-Meslay in France (see 3.2).

transformation of vast expanses of forest and marshland into productive fields and pastures was perhaps the most significant event in medieval European agriculture. The great land clearances begun in the tenth century, indeed as early as the seventh century in some regions, continued through to the fourteenth century in the northern fringes of Germany. Historians have associated them with population growth and the increasing demand for grain.

The Church and magnates controlling the undeveloped land saw this as an opportunity to increase their revenues through taxation, tithes, and rents. Stewards acting on their behalf actively recruited settlers to open up new areas, and on occasion the Church and lords

7.5

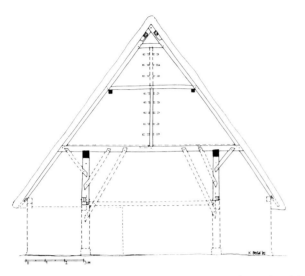 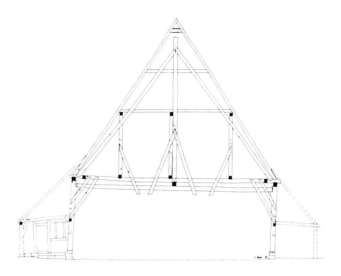

7.6: (*Left*) A cross section of the Höfstetten, a farmhouse from the vicinity of Nürnberg in Germany, which has a square ground plan with aisles on all four sides. It was built in 1367–68, a century before the earliest surviving *hallenhaus*. (*Right*) The roof trusses of the Bauhofscheune, an aisled municipal granary built at Windsheim around 1441, may have been inspired by the carpentry in church roofs.

even pooled their capital in order to build new villages and provide the newcomers with the tools and supplies necessary to get them established.[13]

Dutch and Flemish colonists were especially sought after, because of their expertise in reclaiming marshy areas. The lay brothers of the Cistercian abbey of Les Dunes, founded in 1139, recovered twenty-five thousand acres of farmland from marshy and sandy wastes in Flanders and established twenty-five granges on it. Both colonists and Cistercians helped drain large tracts along the German coastline.[14]

Historically, the colonization of a new region frequently resulted in buildings markedly different from those familiar to the settlers. The buildings erected by Anglo-Saxons when they arrived in England in

the fifth century were distinct from those they had left behind in the Netherlands and northern Germany. When seventeenth- and eighteenth-century pioneers from England, Ireland, and Germany began clearing the forests of North America in their drive westward, the log cabin they built for themselves was unlike any dwelling they had known before. It was in fact a Scandinavian introduction, possibly transmitted to the New World by a small band of Finnish backwoodsmen.[15]

The English researcher J. T. Smith has noted that invasion has been one of the primary factors in the transmission of new ideas, and that the process of diffusion begins with the buildings of those at the upper levels of society before permeating slowly downward as economic circumstances permit.[16] In a sense the Church might be re-

7.7: The grange of Négron at Amboise, Indre-et-Loire, was a dependency of the Benedictine abbey of Marmoutier at Tours. Recently restored, the barn has been variously dated from the thirteenth to the fifteenth century.

7.8: This superb farmhouse at Grothe, near Cloppenburg in Lower Saxony, was built in 1739.

7.9: This aisled stone barn at Juilly, east of Semur-en-Auxois in Burgundy, has both a central wagon door and a loft made of poles for the storage of hay above the nave. Cattle were stalled in the aisle to the right, facing inward, while horses occupied the opposite aisle. The building is of unknown date.

7.10: The tiled roof of an aisled stone barn at Milhac in the Dordogne, has the shallow pitch characteristic of Roman architecture. Inside, the king-post trusses are carried on jowled arcade posts. The opening over the center door provides access to the hayloft above the nave. Livestock are stalled in the aisles.

7.12: A four-bay barn of anchor-beam construction at Usselo, near Enschede in the Netherlands. Although similar in many respects to the New York State aisled barns, it is used chiefly for the storage of excess crops, which can be pitched out through the small door in the jettied gable. It is undated, but is probably from the late eighteenth century.

7.11: The cow in the sunken stall of the broad six-bay barn at Le Puy in the Dordogne faces the threshing floor. Although the loft above the nave has been dismantled, fodder is still stacked in the aisle above the livestock. The arcade posts rest on pad stones.

7.13

7.13, 7.14: The Manoir du Mont-St.-Michel, at Bretteville-sur-Odon in Calvados, Normandy, was a Benedictine priory and dependency of Mont-St.-Michel. The seven-bay barn, built in the second half of the thirteenth century, has two wagon porches in the south side and measures 118 feet by 59 feet (36 m by 18 m). The roof was restored after its destruction in World War II. The stone piers, like those of the Church of Maladrerie St.-Lazare near Beauvais, are octagonal in cross section (see also 9.1).

7.14

7.15: The monospan barn at Doulting, built around 1275, is the oldest of the four surviving barns of Glastonbury Abbey in Somerset, England. Like Bretteville, it has two wagon porches in the side, which reduces its available storage space to 75 percent of the total volume. An interior wall divides the building in half. The separate entries suggest one half may have been intended to hold the crops taken from the abbey's 505-acre *demesne*, which included 357 acres of arable fields, while the other was utilized by the tenants.

7.16

garded as an invasive, albeit peaceful, power. Following the Norman Conquest of England, the more affluent gentry and yeomen began imitating the aisled halls of their new lords and erected aisled barns on their own farms like those they saw on monastic estates.[17]

These estates must have had a considerable impact on the local populations. In the mid-eleventh century, for example, the Benedictine abbey of Ely owned farms in 116 different villages, and peasants living in 200 other villages were in some way dependent upon it. A couple of centuries later, its property had expanded to around 69,000 acres.[18] By the fourteenth century, and no doubt even earlier, landlords in England were actively involved in the maintenance and construction of peasant buildings on their estates.[19]

In Belgium the abbey at Nivelles in Brabant was endowed with 16,000 hectares (around 40,000 acres) after it was founded in 640 A.D. In France during the early ninth century the abbey of St. Germain-des-Pres owned almost 81,000 acres (32,748 hectares), farmed by around 13,300 peasants and their families. An additional 26,500 people lived on lands granted in benefice by the abbey.[20]

In Germany the abbey of Werden owned farms in East Frisia, the Ems district, and the provinces of Drenthe and Twente in the Netherlands. Representatives of the abbot on tours of inspection expected to receive food and shelter at any of the outlying farmhouses, which were spaced some ten kilometers apart.[21] Maintenance work on monastic buildings as well as on *demesne* outbuildings in France, England, and Germany was performed by local carpenters and tenants from the surrounding areas.[22]

While such arguments remain inconclusive, later improvements illustrate just how great an influence nearby market towns had on the development of the *hallenhaus*. For instance, the jettied gables of an urban building indicated the number of its floors, reflecting the affluence of its owner. But jettying applied to the *hallenhaus*, especially to the end visible to the neighbors, was mere decoration since it has only one upper floor for crop storage (see illustration 5.1). The *vierständerhaus*, a variant of the *hallenhaus* equipped with a larger loft (see illustration 5.7, number 3), might appear to be the natural response to a rising demand for cereals during the sixteenth century.

100

7.17

7.16, 7.17: The seven-bay Major Barn at Lenham in Kent stands on a former *demesne* of the Benedictine abbey of St. Augustine's of Canterbury. Built in the fourteenth century as a replacement for other barns torched by an arsonist in 1298, it is 160 feet (48.75 m) long and has a crown-post roof. There are two wagon doors in each side. The aisles are obstructed by low walls and sills, eliminating through passage along them. (See also 8.22.)

7.18, 7.19: The mid-fifteenth-century aisled barn at Buckwell Farm, near Ashford in Kent, was built by a prosperous yeoman who may have been influenced by barns he saw on surrounding monastic estates. The hooded porch protected laden wagons from the rain. Crops are stacked in bays on either side of the transverse threshing floor. (See also 8.26.)

7.19

7.20, 7.21: Anchor-beams span the nave of this side-entry, three-bay barn from the Limburg region of Belgium. The thatched roof is made up of pairs of common rafters joined by collar-ties. The wagon door opening onto the clay threshing floor contains within it a smaller opening for pedestrian traffic. The building dates to 1697 and now stands at the open-air museum at Bokrijk.

7.21

But in fact it was a fifteenth-century development that began in the towns, when the low sidewalls of houses were raised to increase the living space above.[23]

In towns the doors in the sides of buildings had to be eliminated because houses abutted one another with their gables facing the market square or street. The entries were relocated instead at either end, creating a through passage, or *durchgang*.[24] When this practice was later adopted in the *hallenhaus*, the living quarters had to be moved from the rear end and reorganized in the aisles. The same principle operated in aisled barns. By making the doors at each end large enough, a fully laden wagon could be driven into the *diele*, unloaded, and taken out through the far end (see illustration 6.12).

The gradual demise of the *hallenhaus* may be the result of equally unexpected factors such as the introduction of chemical fertilizers in the nineteenth century, which alleviated the necessity for cattle and their manure. The trend may have been further aggravated by industrial pollution as high nitrogen levels began killing off the heather needed in the stalls for *plaggen*.[25]

8.1: The coupled-rafter roof of the mid-twelfth-century Cistercian barn at Warnavillers in Picardy, France (see illustrations 4.7–4.12). Triangular trusses bridge the nave at each pair of stone piers. The vertical *poinçons* simply rest on the tie-beams and thus are not in tension. The roof is stiffened laterally by scissor braces.

Chapter 8

CONSTRUCTION

BUILDING CONSTRUCTION in northwestern Europe during the twelfth and thirteenth centuries reflects two distinctly different traditions. In much of France, notably in Burgundy, which was the hearth of Cluniac and Cistercian monasticism, elements of Roman techniques appear to have been successfully preserved,[1] while elsewhere the indigenous timber architecture sprang from Germanic or Celtic roots.

A remarkable number of French monastic barns besides Warnavillers had masonry arcade piers. Surviving examples include Ardenne, Bretteville-sur-Odon, Maubuisson, Perrières, St.-Lazare-de-Beauvais, Fourcheret, Troussures, and Vaulerent. The Romans preferred masonry because it resists compression better than any other building material. The roofs of a Late Antique papal *horreum* outside Rome and of aisled granaries at the villas of Russi and Vicovaro were all carried on piers of brick or stone.[2]

In *cellaria* and other monastic buildings with vaulted roofs, masonry piers were employed to support the load. Northern visitors to Rome were fascinated by the lavish use of stone columns in buildings and even purchased specimens to bring home. One twelfth-century English traveler marveled at the baths of Diocletian, which had "columns so tall that one cannot throw a small stone as high as the capital. It took a hundred men one year, according to the cardinals, to cut one column into slices."[3]

8.2: Detail of a tie-beam, *poinçon,* and lapped scissor braces.

The roof is the most crucial element of any building. It not only provides essential protection from the weather but requires the most complex carpentry. The Romans understood that a triangle cannot be distorted laterally, unlike a rectangle, and they also recognized the tensile strength of timber. Their triangular roof truss exploited both these features.

The Roman truss consists of a pair of rafters tenoned at their bases into each end of a horizontal tie-beam, thus constraining the rafter feet from spreading outward. A collar-beam keeps them from buckling under the roof load. The rafters are tenoned at their apex into a vertical hanger which extends down to clasp the center of the tie-beam, preventing it from sagging. As a result the tie-beam and hanger are in direct tension, while the collar and rafters are in compression. Because Roman roofs had a low pitch and were often covered with tiles, heavy rafters were usually required.[4]

With the notable exception of the thirteenth-century barn of the Commanderie de Templiers de St.-Vaubourg (see illustrations 9.2–9.4), similar trusses appear in the roofs of virtually all medieval French monastic barns in one form or another, spaced at bay intervals and resting on plates which run over the arcade piers. The hanger, or *poinçon,* supports a ridge piece at the apex. Transverse braces to the principal rafters prevent them from bending, while longitudinal struts to the ridge piece restrain them from overturning. Once in position the

8.3: Cruck-framed buildings are characteristic of highland areas of Britain. The fourteenth-century, ten-bay cruck barn at Leigh Court in Worcestershire is the largest in the country, measuring 100 feet by 27 feet (30.5 m by 8.25 m). The cruck blades are approximately 20 inches by 14 inches (51 cm by 35.5 cm) at their bases. Two porches on the south side open into the third and seventh bays. The manor originally belonged to the Benedictine abbey of Pershore, mentioned in the Domesday survey of 1086.

8.4: Some of the trusses in the roof of the fourteenth-century tithe barn at Bradford-on-Avon in Wiltshire (see 1.7 and 1.8) consist of base crucks surmounted by upper crucks, like the one in the foreground, while others rise unbroken to the ridge.

8.5: The bridled anchor-beam, or *kopbalken*, of the thirteenth-century Grange aux Dimes (tithe barn) at Heurteauville (Seine-Maritime) in Normandy has been reinforced by a pair of beams straddling the arcade plates (see color plate 25).

8.6: Curved wind braces in the porch of the barn at Leigh Court.

trusses are further stabilized longitudinally by purlins placed on cleats attached to the backs of the principal rafters.[5]

Common rafters of a smaller cross section lie across the purlins, and to them is attached the roof covering of tile or thatch. The result is a self-supporting timber superstructure designed to resist racking and lateral distortion. The roof load is transmitted to the trusses and from there to the supporting arcade piers. When repairs become necessary, the common rafters may be removed without disturbing the trusses.

The rafters of the barn at Warnavillers are noteworthy in that they all have the same scantling, or cross section. The arcade piers carry trusses, but none of the intermediate rafters are connected by tie-beams. Instead, the feet of these coupled rafters are secured to a pair

8.7: Wind braces in the open fourteenth-century roof of Brethren's Hall at St. Cross Hospital in Winchester form an elegant design.

8.8: A heavy king-post roof truss with through-purlins in the aisled barn at Gunthwaite Hall near Penistone in South Yorkshire. As in France, the king post is in tension. Built around 1568–1580, the eleven-bay barn measures 163 feet by 44 feet (50 m by 13.5 m). (See also 9.11.)

8.9: Perhaps the most critical joint in a barn occurs at the point where three key timbers, the arcade post, plate, and tie-beam, meet. Here at Gunthwaite carpenters employed the standard English lap-dovetail assembly.

of parallel arcade plates (*sablières*). The builders' concern for lateral stability is clear from the scissor bracing above the nave.[6]

According to Viollet-le-Duc this uniform rafter roof materialized in the twelfth century during the transition from Romanesque to Gothic architecture. Carpenters attempted to lighten the roofs and supporting walls of cathedrals by increasing the roof pitch and simultaneously reducing the thickness of the Roman two-tier roof system. Their solution was to remove the purlins and position the common rafters (*chevrons*) in the same plane as the principal rafters (*arbalétriers*). The wall upon which they rested could thus be made thinner, with the load now distributed evenly along it instead of being transmitted through the principal rafter truss.[7]

Aisled construction was reintroduced to England with the Norman invasion of 1066, for perhaps the first time since the Roman occupation. While it is not uncommon to find masonry piers in buildings like the Great Hall at Winchester (see illustration 9.7) and Oakham Castle (see illustrations 1.16–1.18), in barns they appeared only at Cholsey and Wells.[8] Evidently the local builders felt more comfortable using timber for the posts of monastic barns (see color plate 19).

The technique of roof construction also seems to have followed regional tradition, although the Roman *king-post* truss turns up in northeastern England as exemplified in the sixteenth-century barn at Gunthwaite Hall. Perhaps it originated with Fountains and Rievaulx, two great Cistercian monasteries strongly influenced by Clairvaux, which were established in Yorkshire in the twelfth century.

Viollet-le-Duc remarked that English carpenters were ignorant of a simple principle known since antiquity, namely that the purpose of the tie-beam should be to anchor the feet of the principal rafters rather than to act as a support. Consequently they were obliged to use heavier timbers than their counterparts across the Channel in order to carry the loads placed on them, as in the case of the *crown-post* roofs of barns in southeastern England.[9]

By the twelfth and thirteenth centuries the great monastic barn had already been perfected. Indigenous peasant housing, by comparison, was still relatively crude. To prevent a building like the *hallenhaus* from collapsing, it needed to be supported on posts set deep in the ground. The inherent disadvantage of such earthfast post construction was its brief life span, because damp soil caused the timbers to rot rapidly.

The logical method to increase longevity was to raise the structure off the ground on stone pads (see Prologue illustration), but in order to do so, carpenters had to develop a freestanding timber framework. Attempts seem to have been made in Jutland, southern Denmark, in the late Iron Age, and at native Roman settlements in the southern Netherlands in the second and early third centuries, but they were never fully adopted by the local populations.[10]

The collapse of a Romano-British barn near Chichester, England, around the close of the fourth century may point to a structural deficiency which preoccupied builders for some time. The masonry of the east end was preserved so perfectly where it fell that the excavators were able to deduce the height of the structure and other architectural features, such as the doorway, which was wide enough to admit a cart. Pad stones had been placed along the sidewalls to support timber posts, but the posts had slowly keeled over. In this as in other British buildings of the Roman period carpenters apparently did not know how to stiffen the frame lengthwise with diagonal bracing.[11]

In northern Germany, the transition from earthfast arcade posts to posts resting on stone pads took place gradually, commencing in the eleventh/twelfth century and ending in the fourteenth/fifteenth century. The self-supporting timber frame of the *hallenhaus* that emerged resembled the Gothic cathedral insofar as it was "subdivided into a multitude of equal or homologous parts by means of an all-pervasive skeleton of shafts and arches which act both as divisive and as connective members."[12]

Just as medieval scholars began methodically dividing their texts into chapters, which in turn were split into increasingly smaller conceptual units, so too local carpenters learned to systematically

8.10: The thirteen-bay barn at Frindsbury is, at 210 feet (64 m), the longest in Kent. Built in the fourteenth century, it stood on a *demesne* of St. Andrew of Rochester. Iron bands have been placed around the heads of two of the jowled arcade posts to prevent them from splitting apart (see also 8.21).

8.11: The crown-post roof at Frindsbury is typical of barns in southeastern England. The post rises from the center of the tie-beam to support a purlin running immediately below the collars near the apex of the rafters, the intent being to stiffen the roof and prevent the rafters from overturning.

8.12, 8.13: The roof of a *hallenhaus* is relatively simple. In buildings such as the early eighteenth-century *lös hoes* from Beuningen in Overijssel (8.12), now at the Arnhem open-air museum, widely spaced coupled rafters and collars are commonly used (8.13).

8.13

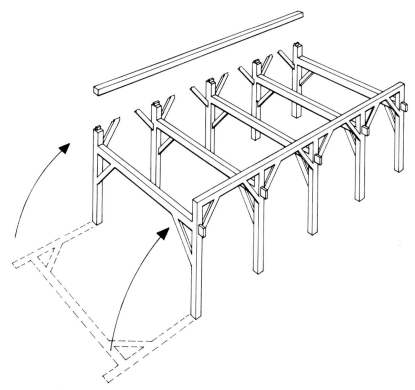

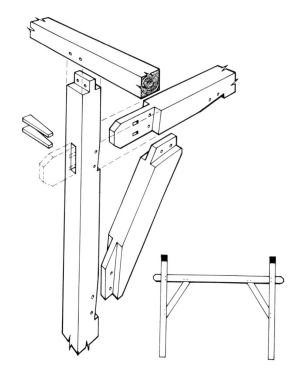

8.14: (*Top left*) Erecting a timber frame of anchor-beam construction. (*Bottom right*) An anchor-beam frame, or bent (from the Dutch word *gebint*). Through-tenons are used in house construction across Europe from Scandinavia to the Spanish Pyrenees, as well as in Japan and Indonesia. Viking beds employed the joint as early as the ninth century. In England it is found in furniture but not in buildings.

partition the space of the peasant farmhouse and barn.[13] The result was a modular structure consisting of cellular bays separated by transverse frames made up of posts, tie-beams, and rafters, stiffened by braces and stabilized longitudinally by sills, plates, and purlins. Perhaps the inspiration for such improvements came from other buildings perfected in an earlier age, which stood not far from the peasants' own holdings. These were the great monastic barns to which peasants brought their tithes.

The language of building disseminated by Roman architects a millennium and a half before the *hallenhaus* may have been adulter-ated by northern dialects, but the Church and State always remained conversant in it as late eighth-century monuments such as Charlemagne's Palatine Chapel at Aachen and the Abbey Gate House at Lorsch clearly demonstrate.[14]

The Diribitorium, built in Rome by Agrippa in 7 B.C., had a roof span of around 100 feet (30.5 m). It was, wrote Cassius Dio in the early third century, "the largest building under a single roof ever constructed." After the roof was consumed in the great fire of 80 A.D., the edifice was left open to the sky, since no trees of sufficient length could be found to replace the timbers destroyed.[15]

8.15: The notch in the anchor beam of a Dutch farmhouse (c. 1750) from Beltrum in Gelderland suggests that the timber previously served as a *dachbalken* (see 8.19). The building is now at the open-air museum in Arnhem.

8.16: An anchor-beam in a wagon shed, from the Stening-Böving farm in the Borken district of Westphalia, terminates in a double tenon. One tenon passes through the corner post and is fastened to the exterior tenon with wooden wedges. The shed, dated 1743, now stands at the open-air museum at Detmold.

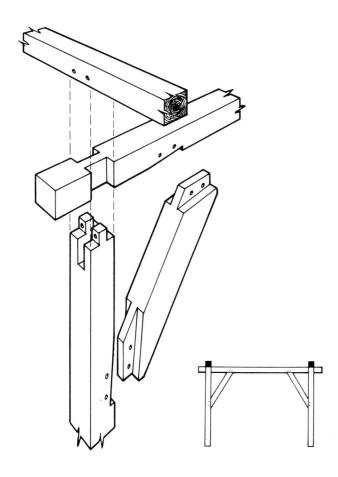

8.17: A bridled anchor-beam, or *kopbalken*, assembly.

8.18: A bridled anchor-beam in the Cistercian barn at Eraine (Oise) in Picardy, which belonged to the abbey of Ourscamp. Mentioned in a document from 1285, the barn measures 147.5 feet by 39.5 feet (45 m by 12 m), and has two porches in the side. It has just one aisle, on the west side of the nave. Since it occurs earlier in building construction this technique may have preceded the anchor-beam.

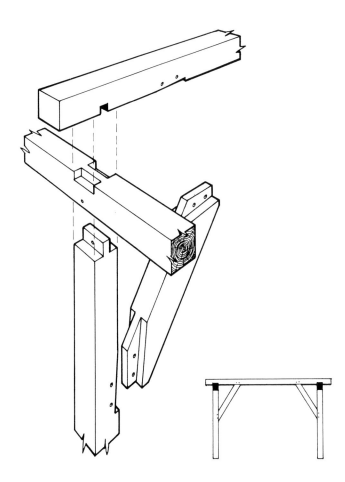

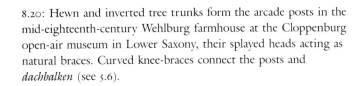

8.19: A *dachbalken* (literally, roof-beam) assembly.

8.20: Hewn and inverted tree trunks form the arcade posts in the mid-eighteenth-century Wehlburg farmhouse at the Cloppenburg open-air museum in Lower Saxony, their splayed heads acting as natural braces. Curved knee-braces connect the posts and *dachbalken* (see 5.6).

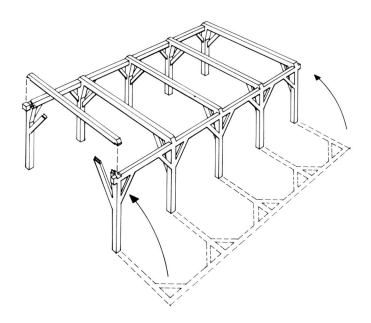

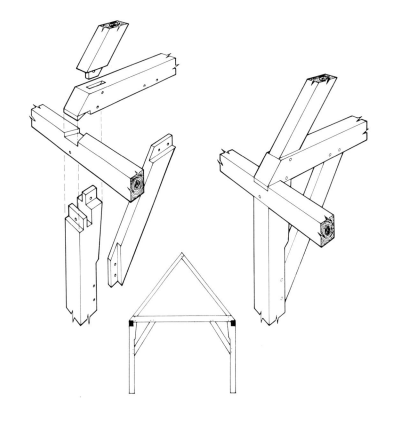

8.21: In the lap-dovetail method of assembly, where the tie-beams straddle the arcade plates to prevent them from spreading apart, the sides of the building must be erected first. A disadvantage of this joint is that as the dovetail on the lower face of the tie-beam shrinks when the timbers dry out, the plates bow outward and the arcade posts sometimes split (see 8.10).

Rome contained a number of buildings of comparable size. For instance, the nave of the Basilica Ulpia in Trajan's Forum measured 80 feet by 260 feet (25 m by 80 m), while that of St. Paul's Outside the Walls was of similar width. North of the Alps Constantine raised a basilica in 310 A.D. at the imperial capital of Trier that rivaled them in grandeur.[16]

Elsewhere in the Empire, as a relief on Trajan's Column (112 A.D.) commemorates, Apollodorus of Damascus designed a bridge which spanned the Danube in a series of timber arches carried on masonry piers 150 feet (46 m) high and spaced 70 feet (21 m) apart.[17] At Rödgen in Germany military engineers erected three enormous timber *horrea* around 11 A.D. in support of Drusus's campaigns across the Rhine, the largest of which, measuring some 155 feet by 97 feet (47.25 m by 29.5 m), must have had multiple aisles. Remains of timber granaries of a lesser scale have been found as far north as Fendoch in Scotland.[18]

By comparison English carpentry did not reach its peak until 1399, when Hugh Herland, King Richard II's master carpenter, completed the grandest feudal hall in Europe at Westminster. Interlocking oak timbers less than 30 feet in length, he successfully raised a cantilevered roof of hammer-beam construction 240 feet long and with an uninterrupted span of 67.5 feet (73 m by 21 m).[19] The structure it replaced, curiously enough, was an aisled hall erected by William Rufus at the close of the eleventh century.

8.22: A lap-dovetail assembly at the head of a splayed arcade post in the fourteenth-century aisled barn at Lenham in Kent. (See also 7.16 and 7.17.)

8.23: A lap-dovetail assembly in the rebuilt fifteenth-century frame of the barn at Parçay-Meslay, Indre-et-Loire, France. (See also color plate 7 and illustrations 3.1–3.5.)

8.24: This arcade post in the Minor Barn on the farm of the royal Cluniac Abbey at Faversham in Kent consists of an upturned forked tree trunk. The building is 86 feet (26 m) long.

124

8.25: A forked tree trunk serves as an anchor-beam in the Saterhaus at the Cloppenburg open-air museum in Lower Saxony, Germany. Two tenons pass through the arcade post and are wedged tight against the outer face.

8.26: When the timbers for a barn are cut and pre-assembled in a builder's yard, they are numbered to assist the carpenter in reassembling the frame. These numerals are on an arcade post and brace in the mid-fifteenth-century aisled barn at Buckwell Farm near Ashford in Kent. (See also 7.18 and 7.19.)

9.1: Masonry arcades flank the nave of the barn at the Manoir du Mont-St.-Michel, at Bretteville-sur-Odon in Normandy (See also 7.13 and 7.14)

Chapter 9

BUILDING MATERIALS

HEN PLINY described in the first century A.D. how his countrymen built elaborate granaries with brick walls a yard thick, in contrast to those "in other places [where] they build their granaries of wood," he did not mean to imply that the Romans suffered from a shortage of timber.[1]

In fact, up to the second century A.D. the Roman army constructed some enormous timber *horrea* along the frontiers of Britain and Gaul, at which time Trajan ordered that they be rebuilt in stone.[2] What led the Romans to abandon timber was not the shortage of it, nor their lack of skill in timber framing. Rather it was the ever-present danger of fire, which, coupled with the discovery of mortar, prompted them to replace timber roofs with ones vaulted in stone.

The Mediterranean was once richly forested, as the Greek writer Theophrastus (c. 370–285 B.C.) admiringly pointed out: "In Syria . . . the cedars . . . are sometimes so large that three men cannot embrace the tree. And in the parks they are even larger and finer. . . . In Cyprus the kings used not to cut the trees, both because they took great care of them and husbanded them, and also because the transport of the timber was difficult. . . . But largest of all, they say, are the trees of Corsica; for whereas silver fir and fir grow in Latium to a very great size . . . these are said to be nothing to the trees of Corsica."[3]

It is astonishing to learn from Pliny that "the largest tree ever seen in Rome . . . was a log of larchwood, 120 feet long and of a uniform thickness of two feet, from which could be inferred the almost incredible height of the rest of the tree by calculating its length to the top."[4] The beam came from the Raetian Alps in the area of Austria and eastern Switzerland.

The roof of Old St. Peter's Basilica in Rome, completed in 377 A.D., is said to have contained a tie-beam 77 feet long by 3 feet thick. A fourteenth-century visitor was moved to write: "I have seen one [roof beam] marked with the name of the builder of the church [Constantine]; it was so huge that all kinds of animals had bored their holes and nests in it. The holes looked like small caverns, many yards long, and gave shelter to thousands of rats."[5] To find such timbers today, one would have to comb the forests of redwoods and Douglas fir along the West Coast of the United States.

When the Romans left northern Europe, the population declined sharply and abandoned fields reverted to forest. Native carpenters continued to build with wood, although during the Carolingian renaissance of the eighth to ninth centuries churches and royal palaces modeled on classical precedents were once more being constructed of stone.[6]

Sources for good timber must have become scarce in France by the mid-twelfth century, because when Abbot Suger needed twelve tall trees for the roof of his church at St. Denis, he was ridiculed. It was considered a miracle when he found what he needed in the valley of Chevreuse.[7]

Fire remained a constant hazard during the Middle Ages, consuming the timber roofs of many great cathedrals and churches including Canterbury, Chartres, Mont St.-Michel, and St.-Riquier. Chartres, for example, burned in 858, 1020, 1030, 1137, and 1194. The substitution of stone for timber not only minimized the danger but instilled a sense of permanence, while the vaulted roofs provided better acoustics for the choirs. Odilo, the abbot responsible for the rebuilding of Cluny in the eleventh century, remarked, "I found an abbey of wood, and I leave it in marble."[8]

The monasteries, particularly the prosperous Cistercian ones, rebuilt their barns for similar reasons. These are the oldest operational

9.2

9.2, 9.4: While the thirteenth-century Templar barn at the Commanderie de St.-Vaubourg at Val-de-la-Haye (Seine-Maritime) in Normandy is sheathed in stone for protection against the elements, the interior is of timber. The five-bay barn, measuring 97 feet by 56 feet (29.5 m by 17 m), has a central wagon door in the end as well as a pedestrian opening in one side. The massive oak posts, set on pad stones, are 20 inches (51 cm) square. Discrepancies in each aisle suggest that the roof has been partially rebuilt. Instead of king-post roof trusses as in other French barns, this one has truncated principal rafters like those in Great Coxwell, England (see 1.3).

9.3: Each arcade post carries double plates, one cantilevered inward above the other.

9.4

129

9.5

9.6

9.5, 9.6: Piers of stone support the roof of the barn of the priory of Perrières, in Calvados, Normandy (see 1.12–1.15).

9.7: Piers of Purbeck marble support the roof of the Great Hall of Winchester Castle in Hampshire, built between 1222 and 1235 and measuring 111 feet by 55 feet (34 m by 17 m). Although stone piers were common in French monastic barns, they were rarely used in English examples. The legend that the round table hanging on the west wall belonged to King Arthur, who lived in the fifth or sixth century, was refuted when it was dated to c. 1250.

9.8 - 9.10: A shell of brick and tile encloses the inner timber frame of the nine-bay barn of the Cistercian abbey of Ter Doest at Lissewege in West Flanders. Built around 1280, its dimensions are approximately 180 feet by 72 feet by 59 feet high (55 m by 22 m by 18 m). The gable walls have blind Gothic arches (see color plate 8). Like Great Coxwell in England (see 1.4) the builders used intermediate trusses between the principal aisled trusses to create unusually wide bays. Stalls for livestock occupy the left aisle.

9.8

9.9

barns in Europe, because their skeletal timber frames have been protected from decay by a sheathing of stone and tile. The late thirteenth-century Cistercian barn of Ter Doest, at Lissewege in Belgium, was constructed of brick instead.

Oak remained the material of choice in medieval England because of its strength and resistance to rot. The earliest surviving timber barns, also constructed in the thirteenth century, are framed in oak and stand at Cressing Temple (see color plate 18) and Coggeshall in Essex. It comes as a surprise, however, to discover that Norwegian

9.10

stave churches of pine are even more ancient, dating back to the mid-twelfth century.[9]

The ancient Greeks also used oak for construction according to Theophrastus, but they preferred silver fir. A house recently torn down in Switzerland contained fir logs (*abies alba*) dendro-dated to 1187 A.D., and several others have successfully withstood weathering since the thirteenth and fourteenth centuries. In Germany more early farmhouses of pine survive than of oak, although the reason for this may simply be that the south, with its coniferous forests, was more densely populated in medieval times than the north.[10]

Curiously, farmhouses in the forested Jura region of Switzerland were built of stone after the seventeenth century, while in adjacent areas they continued to be constructed of logs. This was the result of an edict issued by the bishop of Basel, who prohibited the felling of trees other than for charcoal production.[11] Southeastern Jutland in Denmark was heavily wooded, yet the use of oak was curtailed in houses and barns during the eighteenth century because it was needed by the navy for warships.[12]

A contradictory logic seems to be at work when one finds the English using oak for their barns and imported conifers for their railroad ties, while the reverse is true in the Tyrol. In Japan commoners were permitted to build their farmhouses out of hardwoods such as oak, zelkova, and chestnut, but cypress and cedar were reserved for the nobility. The lesson is not to take traditional assumptions for granted. With the appropriate construction techniques, softwoods are as durable as hardwoods when protected from the weather by overhanging roofs like those of Black Forest farmhouses.[13]

England's rich heritage of timber buildings suggests that the country must have been thickly forested throughout the medieval period. But in fact the Domesday Book, a survey taken twenty years after the Norman invasion, indicates that woodland covered less of England in 1086 (15 percent) than in France today (20 percent). By 1350 this figure had shrunk to 10 percent, yet timber was esteemed so highly that it was transported over considerable distances and even imported from the Baltic countries from the thirteenth century onward.[14]

Timbers from abandoned buildings were commonly reused in new ones and redundant barns were converted into dwellings, evidence that beams of comparable quality were used throughout. In many parts of Europe, buildings were considered to be movable chattels. One advantage of timber-frame construction is that the component members can be readily disassembled and transported elsewhere.[15]

Since it was both wasteful and time-consuming to fell large oaks and saw them into lesser dimensions, English carpenters selected the smallest trees necessary for the job. Woodlands were managed by coppicing, a practice that goes back to Roman times, whereby the stumps of felled trees are allowed to regenerate shoots.

Average-sized barns and houses contained large numbers of young trees, while the main load-bearing timbers for the great barns came from oaks allowed to grow above this underwood, producing relatively straight trunks for the first twenty feet or so. Other large trees came from hedgerows bordering fields and boundary lines. Hazel shoots were interwoven and covered with clay, dung, and horsehair to provide wattle-and-daub panels in the timber walls. The English woodlands, despite their limited size, were always maintained as a renewable resource.[16]

Initially the English colonists in Massachusetts tried to manage their forests with similar care by imposing fines for the unauthorized cutting of trees. John Mackintosh was summoned before the selectmen of Dedham, Massachusetts, in 1664 after flouting the law by gathering timbers for a barn. In Salem, the citizens proclaimed that "henceforward noe sawyer clapboard cleaver or any other person whatsoever shall cutt downe saw or cleave any boards or tymber within our lymits and transport them to other places [because this has already] bared our woods verie much of the best tymber trees of all sorts."[17]

But the seemingly endless bounty of the American wilderness resulted in a reckless abandonment which persists to this day. In the eighteenth century the Swedish botanist Peter Kalm, appalled by the wanton cutting of timber in New Jersey, warned, "People are here

9.11: Chevron-patterned timbers rise above courses of sandstone in the south side of the barn at Gunthwaite Hall in South Yorkshire. (See also 8.8 and 8.9.)

(and in many other places) in regard to wood, bent only upon their own present advantage, utterly regardless of posterity. By these means many swamps are already quite destitute of cedars. . . ."[18]

Don't do as many farmers I have known [pleaded de Crèvecoeur from his home in New York State]. Cut down only the trees that are in your way; for the cold of your long winters, the building and repairing of your barns and sheds, the upkeep of your fences, all require a huge amount of wood. The second generation will regret bitterly that the first destroyed so many trees, something that has already happened in several districts of New Jersey and Connecticut, where, for lack of wood, the value of the land has diminished considerably.

And even if one considers the forests only as an ornament, as a magnificent robe with which nature in its kindness has covered this continent, are they not beautiful and majestic? How can one keep from venerating these gigantic pines, which no amount of human skill and cultivation can ever replace? Those oaks, whose origin is much more ancient than that of our greatest cities? This respect for the forests and the beautiful trees is so natural that . . . a landowner, after some years of possession, is instinctively more moved, more flattered, on going through his woods than in crossing his fields.[19]

His appeal was never heeded. Like the huge firs and cedars of the Mediterranean described by Theophrastus over two millennia ago, these giants too have all but vanished today. The massive timbers in abandoned Dutch-built barns are mute survivors of a plundered land.

9.12: The fifteenth-century stone tower at Masse (Aveyron) in the Rouergue, built by the Cistercian abbey of Bonneval, served as both dwelling and granary. (See also color plate 26.)

9.13, 9.14: A pair of curious stone reliefs adorn a doorway at the grange of Gaussan (Aude), which once belonged to the Cistercian abbey of Fontfroide. (See also color plate 27.)

10.1: The roof of the late fourteenth-century barn at Pilton in Somerset was destroyed by fire in 1963. All but forgotten after six centuries of service, its empty shell now stands open to the sky. (See also 1.11.)

138

EPILOGUE

THE SEARCH INTO the origin of aisled barns remains about as elusive as the quest for truth. There are moments when enlightenment appears to recede in direct proportion to the time spent in pursuit of it. The threads of evidence are fragile, and the fabric into which they are fashioned is diaphanous at best. As a scholar once cautioned, there has never been any shortage of theories; the trouble has been to anchor theory to the solid ground of historical fact.[1] For the time being, there is no neat solution.

The information I have drawn upon is based upon the work of archaeologists and anthropologists, architectural historians and agricultural historians, ecologists, ethnographers, geographers, farmers, and builders. Those with whom I have spoken have been immensely generous in the sharing of their knowledge. My role was to question why, and theirs to provide the answers. Inevitably, however, the illumination provided by one source would be dimmed by another. Unambiguous though it might seem, the barn remains something of an enigma.

Appendix

STORING THE HARVEST

ONE OF THE GREAT advantages of grain over other foodstuffs is that it remains edible and nutritious over lengthy periods of time, but only if properly stored. Until stockpiles can be replenished the following harvest, or even later in the event of crop failure, they need to be carefully protected from spoilage. Consequently barns and granaries are designed to keep the contents cool and dry, with space set aside for processing them by threshing and winnowing the ears. Ideas on appropriate conservation methods advanced by Roman agronomists two millennia ago astonishingly do not seem to have been much improved upon by farmers right up to the twentieth century.[1]

In Roman Italy, cereals were usually threshed shortly after reaping and the grain placed in a granary. "If, however, the heads only are cut off," Columella wrote in the first century A.D., "they may be carried into the *horreum* and then, during the winter, be beaten out with flails or trodden out by cattle."[2]

Interestingly, the Britons had a similar custom. Writing around 56 B.C., Diodorus of Sicily noted that "the method they employ of harvesting their grain crops is to cut off no more than the heads and store them away in roofed granges, and then each day they pick out the ripened heads and grind them, getting in this way their food."[3]

When harvesting their crops, the Romans often severed the stalks in the middle. Peasants in northern Europe followed a similar procedure during the medieval period, carrying the sheaves to the barn and threshing them over the winter when there was little else to do (see color plates 4 and 5). The remaining stubble might be turned over to animals to graze on or else set afire to eliminate the weeds and return some nutrients to the soil. Straw was also used for cattle litter and for

thatching roofs, rye being the most durable variety.

Columella's advice to farmers was to reap "when the crop is . . . golden yellow, before the grains have entirely hardened . . . so that the grain may grow larger on the floor and in the stack rather than in the field." The stalks were less brittle and easier to cut at this stage, and the seeds less likely to drop off. The grain could continue to extract nutrients while in the sheaf, and Varro argued it would also be sweeter to the taste. Pliny noted that grain "if stored in the ear . . . hardly ever suffers injury," which accords with contemporary research. Removal of the seed husk by threshing probably exposes it to greater insect and fungal attack.[4]

Roman writers differed amongst themselves on the best way to store grain. Varro was in favor of granaries elevated above the ground, while Vitruvius thought the grain should be piled up on a well-sealed concrete floor. Columella suggested that "grain, hay . . . and other fodder, should be stored in lofts," adding that if the weather were not so damp, "it would be possible to keep grain even buried underground, as in certain districts across the sea." He may not have been aware of it, but such pits had been used by native tribes in northern Europe since prehistoric times. Pliny quoted Varro as saying that "wheat so stored lasts fifty years."[5]

Although figures fluctuate dramatically, in third-world countries today anywhere from 10 percent to 50 percent of crops is lost annually to damage from rodents, mold, bacteria, insects, and spontaneous combustion.[6] In medieval Europe, the spoilage may have been equally severe.

Since time immemorial granaries have been set on capped piers of stone or timber to keep rodents out. Openings were incorporated into barns to entice natural predators such as owls and cats to take up residence within. Traces of soot on the walls of some Roman granaries in England suggest attempts were made to fumigate them,[7] and smoke from an open hearth in the *hallenhaus* may have served the same purpose.

When grain is stored in bulk it respires, creating heat within the pile and setting up a convection current. Cool air adjacent to the walls of the granary settles at the base and then rises through the warm mass in the center, picking up moisture and depositing it as condensation on the top surface. This produces ideal conditions for concentrated fungal growth. Damaged grain is particularly vulnerable to mold and insects. Accumulated pockets of debris impede ventilation and provide further nourishment to fungi.[8] For long-term storage the Romans sometimes winnowed grain twice after threshing it, even passing it through a sieve in order to get rid of impurities.[9]

Insects such as the grain weevil, the saw-toothed grain beetle, and the flour mite commonly feed on grain, damaging the germs and releasing heat, carbon dioxide, and moisture. This stimulates fungal growth which in turn provides food for some of the insects. The grain supply not only becomes contaminated with carcasses but the insects' eggs can survive for extended periods in crevices within the granary while it is empty, hatching out once the space is refilled. Insect activity can be curtailed by keeping the temperature below 17° C.

The Romans tried to eliminate potential hiding places by cementing the floors and plastering the walls of their *horrea*, then sprinkling olive lees (*amurca*) over them to deter weevils and other vermin.[10] Cato recommended *amurca* as a repellent as early as 160 B.C. Vitruvius wrote that "rooms for grain should be set in an elevated position and with a northern or northeastern exposure. Thus the grain will not be able to heat quickly, but, being cooled by the wind, keeps a long time. Other exposures produce the corn weevil and the other little creatures that are wont to spoil the grain."[11]

Fungi that colonize and spoil cereals are of two types, those that thrive in the field and others that only develop in storage. When the relative humidity exceeds 65 to 70 percent, microbial activity begins to release heat, which in combination with that produced by the grain itself eventually raises the temperature above 40° C and destroys the seed. Here again, storing grain in a cool, dry environment is the key to preventing mold growth. In northern Europe, grain will keep up to eight months at a moisture content of 18 percent and a temperature range of 5° to 10° C, and for even longer periods if the moisture level can be further reduced to 13 percent or 14 percent.

Pliny noted how "some people recommend building elaborate granaries [*horrea*] with brick walls a yard thick, and moreover filling them from above and not letting them admit draughts of air or have any window; others say they should only have windows facing northeast and north." He may have been facetious when he prescribed hanging up "a toad by one of its longer legs at the threshold of the barn before carrying the corn into it."[12] It also helped to store grain in sacks or on stalks in sheaves, because the spaces between them allowed better aeration.

All crops, particularly hay, can overheat if improperly stored, and spontaneous combustion still destroys thousands of barns each year. Its causes have been puzzled over for centuries. Columella recommended that "hay be gathered neither when very dry nor . . . while still green—in the one case because it is no better than straw if it has lost all its sap, and in the other because, if it has kept too much . . . it rots in the loft and often, when it becomes heated . . . breeds fire and starts a blaze." For this reason, wrote Vitruvius in the first century B.C., "barns [*horrea*] for grain, hay, and spelt . . . should be built apart from the farmhouse, so that farmhouses may be better protected against danger from fire."[13]

The Elizabethan philosopher Sir Francis Bacon had his own theory for the phenomenon: "All herbs and green and moist vegetables seem to contain some secret heat, though so small as to be imperceptible to the touch in small portions; but when many are joined, and close shut up together, so that their spirit cannot breathe out into the air, but the parts must mutually foment and cherish each other, a manifest heat is produced, and sometimes a flame if the matter is disposed thereto."[14]

In order to store hay safely it needs to be dried below a 20 percent moisture content. Otherwise mold, bacteria, and enzymes will flourish, thereby lowering its nutritional value and also raising the temperature through their respiration. Once above 38° C a chemical reaction occurs, in which amino acids and sugar combine to elevate the temperature still further, frequently resulting in spontaneous ignition and the destruction of the barn.[15]

The layout of an aisled barn provided several options for crop storage. Frequently the wagon moved down the nave and the harvest was unloaded into the aisles on either side or, in the case of the *hallenhaus,* it was pitched into the loft above (see illustration 5.7). Alternatively, since the nave itself had the greatest capacity, one aisle became a through passageway and the harvest was laid up in the main body of the barn (see illustrations 2.4 to 2.6). A third method, common in England, was to have cross-passages in the sides of the building. These areas, made of stone, timber, or tamped earth, also doubled as threshing floors (see illustrations 1.8, 6.5, and 6.11).

An unusual method of stacking the sheaves in English barns involved the use of a docile old horse, or goaf, to tread it down. A boy guided the animal as the pile grew taller until it neared the roof and could go no farther, at which point a rope was passed around a beam and fastened to the goaf so that it could be slid gently to the ground. Once, early in the nineteenth century, a horse that had been left overnight atop an unfinished stack in the Barley Barn, at Cressing Temple in Essex (see color plate 18), had disappeared by the following morning and was presumed stolen. However, someone later heard a whinny from a crevice where it had slipped. After being rescued the unfortunate beast was led to a nearby pond, whereupon it drank so greedily it died.[16]

CHAPTER NOTES

Chapter 1

1. Stoepker, pp. 199–218; Jaap Schipper, "Rural Architecture: The Zaan Region of the Province of North Holland" (*New World Dutch Studies*, Roderic Blackburn, editor, Albany, 1987, pp. 181–182); and John A. Hostetler, *Amish Society* (3rd edition, Johns Hopkins University Press, 1980, pp. 208–210). The point is well illustrated in an Ottonian painting, "Adoration of the Kings" from the Trèves Stadtbibliothek, reproduced in Adolph Goldschmidt, *German Illumination* (Paris, 1928, Vol. 2, plate 68).
2. Leroux; and Viollet-le-Duc, *Dictionnaire raisonné*, Vol. 1, "Architecture monastique."
3. See Berger, pp. 117, 118.
4. Paul Léon, *Les Monuments Historiques—conservation restauration* (Paris, 1917, illustration on p. 41).
5. See Carter; and Turner, pp. 43–45, 168–172.
6. Now reerected at the Fränkisches Freilandmuseum at Bad Windsheim. See Bedal, *Fachwerk vor 1600 in Franken*, pp. 450–453; Helm, pp. 131–134 and plates 42–43; and Walter Horn, unpublished paper in the collection of the Getty Center for the History of Art and the Humanities, California, Archive No. 920089.
7. Horn, "Survival, Revival, Transformation," pp. 714–715.
8. For a definition see Krautheimer, pp. 20–21. See also Philippe Ariés and Georges Duby, *A History of Private Life: From Pagan Rome to Byzantium* (Vol. 1, Harvard University Press, 1987, pp. 334–339); and Boëthius and Ward-Perkins, pp. 127–131.
9. See John T. Smith, "Romano-British Aisled Houses"; Morris, pp. 43–44, 55–65; Todd; Drack; Slofstra, pp. 143, 170; and Bloemers, pp. 172, 173.
10. Boëthius and Ward-Perkins, p. 283, fig. 108; Meiggs, *Roman Ostia*, p. 280; Rickman, *Roman Granaries;* Manning, "Roman Military Timber Granaries"; Manning, *Fortress Excavations;* and Gentry.

Chapter 2

1. The analogy to oil was brought up by L. Casson in "The Role of the State in Rome's Grain Trade" (in *The Seaborne Commerce of Ancient Rome. Studies in Archaeology and History,* Memoirs of the American Academy in Rome, Vol. 36, 1980, pp. 21–34); and Spurr, p. ix. Cuneiform texts dating to the mid-fourth millennium B.C. have been found at the Uruk 4 settlement in southern Mesopotamia. See also Schwartz, "The Ninevite V Period"; and Schwartz and Curvers, "Tell al-Raqā'i 1989 and 1990."
2. See Hole; Reed, p. 143; and Katz and Voigt.
3. John Noble Wilford, "Collapse of Earliest Known Empire Is Linked to Long, Harsh Drought" (*New York Times*, August 24, 1993).
4. Garnsey, pp. 28–29.
5. Ibid., p. 244.
6. The figure varies according to the source. Garnsey states that 6 Roman *modii* = 40 kg, giving a total of some 294,000 tons. Rickman, *Corn Supply,* states that 1 ton of wheat = approx. 150 *modii*, giving a total of 266,667 tons.
7. The information above is taken from Garnsey; and Rickman, *Corn Supply*.
8. Rickman, *Roman Granaries*, p. 5, and *Corn Supply,* p. 23. See also Meiggs, *Roman Ostia,* p. 280, fig. 22, and p. 281, fig. 23.

9. Rickman, *Corn Supply,* p. 187.
10. *Encyclopedia Britannica,* 1973 edition.
11. A similar practice seems to have occurred during the later Roman Empire; see Percival, pp. 121, 122.
12. Gregory of Tours, Book VII. 45.
13. Rickman, *Roman Granaries,* pp. 156–157.
14. Horn and Born, *Plan of St. Gall,* Vol. 3, p. 105.
15. Duby, pp. 45, 123.
16. Horn and Born, *Plan of St. Gall,* Vol. 1, pp. 344–345.
17. Duby, pp. 25–27, 99–103; Titow; and Dyer, *Standards of Living,* pp. 126–127.
18. Lamond, p. 71. See also the Appendix, which deals with crop storage.
19. Groenman van Waateringe, pp. 147–156.
20. Cooter. See also Peter Reynolds, "Slash and Burn Experiment."
21. Le Goff, pp. 236–237.
22. Ibid., p. 235.
23. Ibid., pp. 234, 237–240; and Duby, p. 124.
24. Le Roy Ladurie, pp. 246–256; and Gottfried, pp. 22–25.
25. Le Roy Ladurie, pp. 46–47.
26. Ibid., p. 13.
27. Gottfried, pp. 28–29.
28. Ibid., pp. 129–134.
29. Ibid., p. 87.
30. Dyer, *Standards of Living,* pp. 240–241.
31. Dyer, "English Peasant Buildings."
32. de Crèvecoeur, *Sketches,* p. 141, and *Eighteenth-Century Travels,* p. 45.
33. Stadtfeld, p. 24.

Chapter 3

1. Wightman, pp. 299, 311.
2. Le Goff, p. 29.
3. Ibid., pp. 80, 121, 126.
4. Braunfels, pp. 19–20; Horn, "On the Origins of the Medieval Cloister," p. 43; and Percival, pp. 197, 198.
5. Wightman, p. 111. St. Augustine himself once studied at Cassiciacum, a monastery in Lombardy that originally may well have been a villa; see Percival, p. 197.
6. Viollet-le-Duc, *Discourses on Architecture* (English translation by Henry Van Brunt, Boston, 1895, pp. 260–263). See also Percival, chapter 9, "Villas, Churches and Monasteries."
7. Horn, "On the Origins of the Medieval Cloister," p. 42; and Horn and Born, *Plan of St. Gall,* Vol. 1, p. 245 and figs. 198, 199.
8. Percival, p. 171; Wightman, pp. 210–211, 215, 263, 265, 305, 306, 309–311; Dopsch, pp. 186–189; Rösener, p. 17. See also Roymans, *Tribal Societies,* pp. 268–269; and Bloemers.

9. The takeover of a former imperial estate by Franks is noted in Wightman, p. 310. On the tripartite nature of villas see Columella Book I. VI. 1; Percival, chapter 4; and Rossiter.

10. Braunfels, p. 21; Wightman, pp. 295, 299; and Percival, pp. 178, 179, 183–199.

11. Rickman, *Roman Granaries*, p. 316; Boëthius and Ward-Perkins, p. 520, fig. 196; and Hinz, "Einfahrtstor und Erntebergung," p. 121, fig. 2, and p. 122, fig. 3.

12. Percival, pp. 183–199; Duby, pp. 55, 81, 434; Marc Bloch, *French Rural History*, pp. 2, 99; Koebner, pp. 35–36, 44; and Parain, pp. 126–127.

13. Viollet-le-Duc, *Dictionnaire raisonné*, Vol. 1, "Architecture monastique," pp. 241–312. See also Braunfels, p. 47; and Conant, pp. 82, 107.

14. This translation is adapted from Duby, p. 364; and Horn and Born, *Plan of St. Gall*, Vol. 2, p. 41. In the Netherlands and Germany today, a granary is still referred to respectively as a *spieker* or *speicher* (from *spica*, an ear of cereal), while a barn is called a *schuur* or *scheune*.

15. Wightman, p. 264.

16. Ibid., p. 310; Percival, pp. 129, 138, 145; Theuws, "Landed Property," pp. 313–318; Slofstra, p. 182; and Rösener, p. 17.

17. Constable; and Charles W. Jones. For the tithe system in Sicily, see Rickman, *Corn Supply*, pp. 37–42.

18. Duby, p. 43.

19. Reynolds, *Ancient Farming*; and Roymans, *Tribal Societies*, pp. 95–115.

20. Fussell, p. 39; Percival, pp. 150–152; and Wightman, pp. 119–128.

21. Fussell, p. 51; and Duby, pp. 23–24, 88–89.

22. Roymans, *Tribal Societies*, p. 104.

23. Fussell, pp. 51, 52.

24. Ganshof and Verhulst, "Medieval Agrarian Society," p. 330.

25. Duby, pp. 65–87, 391–395.

26. Ganshof and Verhulst, "Medieval Agrarian Society," pp. 292–296.

27. For a concise account of the Cistercian movement, see Braunfels, pp. 67–110.

28. Personal communication from Terryl N. Kinder. Viollet-le-Duc, in his *Dictionnaire raisonné*, Vol. 1, p. 265, gives an estimated figure of 8,000 to 10,000 barns. For France alone at the start of the thirteenth century, Walter Horn estimates there were 5,000 to 10,000 Cistercian barns. See Horn and Born, *Plan of St. Gall*, Vol. 3, p. 111.

29. Information in this and succeeding paragraphs is largely taken from Berman, *Medieval Agriculture*.

30. See for example Kidson; and Duby, pp. 88–89.

31. See Horn and Born, "Water Power."

32. Notker, Book 1. 28 (in Einhard and Notker the Stammerer); and Mark, pp. 98–100.

33. Braunfels, pp. 71, 89.

Chapter 4

1. Columella, Book I. VI. 24; and Cato and Varro, Varro, Book I. XIII. 5 and I. LI. 2. For accounts of Roman farming techniques, see Spurr; and White, *Roman Farming*.

2. Rossiter, p. 21 and fig. 5A.

3. Vitruvius, Book VI.VI.5; Varro, Book I. XI. 2 and I. LVII. 1–3; Columella, Book I. VI. 7, I. VI. 9, I. VI. 12–13, I. VI. 16, and II. XX. 3; and Pliny the Elder, V. LXIII. 301–303. A vaulted ceiling is mentioned by Columella in Book I. VI. 12.

4. See Columella, Book I. VI. 9 and 10. Agricultural scenes from Tunisian mosaics are discussed and illustrated in Précheur-Canonge. The dates attributed to the mosaics

have been revised on the advice of Dr. Margaret Alexander.

5. See Carter. Ahrens, p. 29, fig. 14, illustrates a Carolingian funerary chapel, while Braunfels, p. 33, shows the Chapel of Our Lady and Church of St. Benedict at St. Riquier.

6. The first scene ("Jungfrauenspiegel") comes from the *Speculum virginum* by Konrad Hirsau, in the collection of the Rheinisches Landesmuseum, Bonn, No. 15328. The scene from Genesis 41: 45–48 is from a *Bible Moralisée*, in the collection of the Bodleian Library, Oxford, MS. Bodl. 270b, fol. 28[R].

7. Dimier, "Les belles granges cisterciennes," pp. 49–61. Dimier may have been referring to the *Cartulaire de l'Abbaye de Notre Dame d'Ourscamp*, dating to the year 1156 (see next note).

8. Achille Peigné-Delacourt, "Cartulaire de l'Abbaye de Notre Dame d'Ourscamp" (*Mémoires de la Société des Antiquaires de Picardie*, Vol. 16, 1866, p. 190); and Horn, "Great Tithe Barn of Cholsey," p. 22.

9. Horn and Born, "Buildings in the Domesday of St. Paul's Cathedral." See also Weller, *Grangia et Orreum*.

10. Sources: *Dictionary of Greek and Roman Antiquities*, by W. Smith (2 vols., London, 1890); *Ainsworth's Dictionary, English and Latin*, by Robert Ainsworth (London, 1873); and *Harper's Latin Dictionary, founded on the Translation of Freund's Latin-German Lexicon* (E. A. Andrews, editor, New York, 1907). See also Rickman, *Roman Granaries*, p. 1. For *horrea* used for the storage of wine, see Meiggs, *Roman Ostia*, pp. 274–275 and plate XXVI; and Lepper and Frere, Plate V, Scene i, and Plate VI, Scene ii. Excavations indicate that occasionally a Roman-built cellar was later converted into a church or chapel; see Wightman, p. 293; and Percival, p. 186.

11. Horn, "On the Origins of the Medieval Cloister," pp. 34–35; and Horn and Born, *Plan of St. Gall*, Vol. II, p. 278, fig. 478.A.

12. Dom Milley, *Vue de l'abbaye de Clairvaux* (gravure by Lucas, 1708, Bibliothèque nationale, Estampes, Paris). The *granarium* originally appears to have been a dormitory for lay brothers. Details of the *Cellarium et Granaria majora* appear in Fowler, pp. 1–5 and plates 3–6; Musso and Miguet; and in an undated paper by Morehart. For roof vaults in granaries, see Columella I. VI. 12. The buildings at Clairvaux now serve as a high-security prison. Vauclair, in the diocese of Laon, also possessed a spectacular two-story, two-aisled vaulted grange that was erected in the thirteenth century. See Lenoir, pp. 411–412.

13. Lekai, p. 212; Graves, pp. 63–70; Platt; and Leroux, pp. 17–23.

14. J. T. Fowler, *Extracts from the Account Rolls of the Abbey of Durham from the Original MSS* (3 vols., Surtees Society, Durham, 1898, 1899, 1901, Vol. I, p. 93); and Sussex Record Society, Vol. 65, 1967, p. 80.

15. Horn and Born, *Plan of St. Gall*, Vol. 1, pp. 326, 333.

16. See Horn and Born, *Plan of St. Gall*, Vol. 3, p. 111, and *Barn of the Cistercian Grange of Vaulerent*, p. 29, plate XIX; Viollet-le-Duc, *Dictionnaire raisonné*, Vol. 1, p. 275, fig. 10; and Morehart, pp. 19–20.

17. Chouquer and de Klijn, p. 285; and Todd, p. 370, fig. 1. A barn with an even number of aisles of equal width, such as the six-aisled example at Clairvaux, implies one row of piers running down the longitudinal axis of the building, supporting the roof at the ridge. This is exactly what occurs in a number of two-aisled monastic buildings, including the *cellier* of Clairvaux at Dijon and the *forge* at the abbey of Fontenay; see Dimier, "Granges, celliers et bâtiments." Nor is it inconsistent with Roman practice in Italy, as, for example, the four-aisled granary of Vicovaro, measuring some 100 feet by 50 feet (29.5 m by 14.8 m), and the two-aisled storerooms at Casalotto and Pratella, reproduced in Rossiter, p. 44, fig. 13B, and p. 58, figs. 15, 59. For ridgepost roofs in

French vernacular architecture, see Bans and Bans, "Continental Roofs."

18. Neil Stratford, Keeper of Medieval Antiquities at the British Museum, questions Kenneth Conant's reconstruction of Cluny II. The dimensions of the cellar are given in *Consuetudines monasticae, Consuetudines Farvensis* (Bruno Albers, editor, Freiburg, 1900, lib. II, cap. I, pp. 137–139). The visit to the storehouse was described by an unknown traveling companion of Peter Damian in *Monumenta Germaniae Historica, Scriptores,* Vol. 30, ii, p. 1043.

19. See Horn and Born, *Plan of St. Gall,* Vol. 2, p. 215.

20. Some scholars suggest Horn's measurements should be reviewed in light of the article by Kidson. The barns on the royal estate at Annappes are discussed in Chapter 3, p. 42.

21. Gregory of Tours, Books IV. 1, VII. 37, and X. 1.

22. Widrig, *Ancient Roman Villa Gardens,* and *Excavations on the Ancient Via Gabina.*

23. Gregory of Tours, Book II. 24.

24. Einhard and Notker the Stammerer, pp. 118–119.

25. Rickman, *Roman Granaries,* p. 316; Boëthius and Ward-Perkins, p. 520, fig. 196; and Hinz, "Einfahrtstor und Ernteber.gung," p. 121, fig. 2, and p. 122, fig. 3.

26. See John T. Smith, "Romano-British Aisled Houses"; Morris, pp. 43–44, 55–65; Percival, pp. 135–137; Wightman, p. 114; Rossiter; Todd; Drack; Slofstra, pp. 143, 170; and Bloemers, pp. 172, 173.

27. J. T. Smith believes that excavated Saxon halls prior to the Conquest have been either wrongly interpreted as being aisled or else incorrectly dated. Archaeological results in Germany and the Netherlands appear to bear him out. Basilican churches of the eighth/ninth century, such as Brixworth and Cirencester, are an exception and reflect a strong Classical influence (see Gem).

Chapter 5

1. Zimmermann, "Ernteberghung in Rutenberg und diemen aus archäologischer und volkskundlicher sicht" (in *Néprajzi Értesítő,* LXXI–LXXIII, 1989–1991, Budapest, 1991), and "The 'Helm.'" In some regions, hay was kept in the loft and the cereals in stacks outside (see Hekker).

2. A good example, dating from c. 1565, now stands at the Westphalian open-air museum in Detmold, Germany. It comes from the Schulte Brüning farm in the district of Warendorf.

3. Fokkens and Roymans, pp. 1–19.

4. The Huijts book presents a reconstruction of the buildings excavated by the Dutch archaeologist H. T. Waterbolk.

5. Fokkens and Roymans, p. 16 and p. 44, fig. 3.

6. Zimmermann, "Roman Iron Age Settlement at Flögeln," p. 154.

7. This argument by Haio Zimmermann and other archaeologists is based upon excavated bone deposits. It is disputed by Heinz Ellenberg, a professor of plant ecology at Göttingen University, who asserts that the cattle were hardy enough to survive outdoors except in the severest weather, and able to digest heather on the moorlands. See also Reynolds, *Ancient Farming,* p. 24; and Percival, p. 151.

8. Zimmermann, "Roman Iron Age Settlement at Flögeln," p. 160.

9. For an account of turf fertilizing using *plaggen,* see Heidinga, pp. 91–92.

10. Zimmermann, verbal communication.

11. Harsema, pp. 204–205; and Zimmermann, *Probleme der Küstenforschung im Südlichen Nordseegebiet.* For an attempted reconstruction of the evolutionary sequence, see Huijts.

12. Zimmermann, verbal communication; and Beresford, pp. 23–24.

13. Harsema.

14. This is not the case in the *vierständerhaus,* a variant of the *hallenhaus,* in which the rafters are unbroken from ridge to outer wall plate. Lean-tos, creating an aisle on one or both sides of otherwise monospan buildings, were added to sixteenth-century barns in Kent, England, and in nineteenth-century field barns in the vicinity of Ballenberg in Switzerland. See, for example, Martin and Martin, Vol. 3, pp. 50–76.

Chapter 6

1. Grant, chapter 18, pp. 174–178.

2. Cohen, "How Dutch," pp. 43–60.

3. Stokes, p. 952.

4. Gehring, p. 48.

5. Jameson.

6. See Fitchen, the first serious study of the three-aisled barn in America.

7. Parkman, p. 563.

8. Talbot, p. 298.

9. Danckaerts, p. 58.

10. *Museumsdorf Cloppenburg* (guide to the Niedersächsisches Freilichtmuseum, 1988, pp. 116–117).

11. Conversation with Heinz Ellenberg, professor of plant ecology at the University of Göttingen, who was born in 1913 and spent his childhood in a *hallenhaus.* He remembers the scent of *plaggen* vividly.

12. *Early Records of the City and County of Albany and Colony of Rensselaerswyck* (Albany, New York, 1916, Vol. 2, pp. 153–154).

13. Ibid., Vol. 3, p. 425.

14. Martin and Martin, Vol. 3, pp. 124–127.

15. Kalm, p. 118.

16. An eighteenth-century date for the aisled barn is given by Hagens, *Boerderijen in Twente,* pp. 21–25, 142. The ground plans of early monospan barns are illustrated in Hessing, p. 44, fig. 3. See also Maschmeyer.

17. See Larson. Aisled barns of independent origins can be found in Louisiana (see Comeaux); in Maine (Hubka, pp. 52–53, 58–60); in Delaware (Herman, pp. 72–73, 202–203); in Tennessee (Kniffen, p. 18); in Virginia, Missouri, North Carolina, Kansas, Ohio, Iowa, Michigan, and Utah (Noble, pp. 2–3, 9–13, 59, 138, 169). Aisled barns directly derived from those built by Dutch and German settlers in New York State spread north into Ontario, Canada (Arthur and Witney, p. 48). Walter Horn photographed aisled barns in California and adjacent states until ill health curtailed his work.

Chapter 7

1. See Hinz, "Einfahrtstor und Ernteberghung," and "Zur Vorgeschichte der Niederdeutschen Halle." Heidinga, Zimmermann, Bedal, Fred Kaspar, and Ellenberg have each indicated support for this view in personal conversations. Waterbolk, on the other hand, believes the *hallenhaus* evolved independently of external influence.

2. Zimmermann, *Die früh- bis hochmittelalterliche wüstung Dalem gem. langen-neuen-walde,* p. 42, fig. 4.

3. See Stoepker. The archaeologist H. T. Waterbolk, in a verbal communication, believes that church architecture simply reflected the local domestic building tradition, rather than the reverse situation.

4. See Slofstra.

5. See Theuws, "Landed Property."

6. The viewpoint expressed by Frans Theuws.

7. An opinion put forward by Nico Roymans.

8. The Höfstetten and the Bauhofscheune have been reerected at the Fränkisches Freilandmuseum at Bad Windsheim. See Bedal, *Fachwerk vor 1600 in Franken*, pp. 30, 201–203, 450–453; and Helm, pp. 131–134 and plates 42–43).

   A cityscape by the Florentine painter Biagio di Antonio (1476–1504), *The Story of Joseph*, at New York's Metropolitan Museum of Art (No. 32.100.69), shows figures bearing sacks (of grain?) emerging from what appears to be an aisled municipal granary.

9. Bedal, verbal communication.

10. Leroux.

11. See Bans and Bans, "Hallenhäuser und Hallenscheunen in Frankreich," pp. 151–181; Meirion-Jones; Ministère des Affaires Culturelles, *Landes: canton Peyrehorade;* various articles by Lassure (see bibliography); Schweizer Baudokumentation, "Maisons rurales dans le Haut-Jura"; and Flores.

   See also Comeaux, which deals with the aisled Cajun barn of Louisiana, a type that the author suggested was introduced by Germans who had settled west of the Mississippi Delta in 1721 and was subsequently adopted by the French. It now appears as though the barn may well have been brought over by the French themselves.

   Three-aisled barns also exist in Norway, Denmark, Hungary, Romania, and no doubt in other European countries. See, for example, Gjaerder; Engqvist; Szentendre Open Air Museum, p. 46; and Ispir.

12. Viollet-le-Duc, *Dictionnaire raisonné,* Vol. 6, pp. 45, 46.

13. Duby, pp. 65–87, 391–398; Koebner; Ganshof and Verhulst, "Medieval Agrarian Society," pp. 291–296; and Rösener, pp. 34–39.

14. Duby, pp. 121, 394–395; Rösener, pp. 227–228; and Lekai, p. 211.

15. See, for example, Harold R. Shurtleff, *The Log Cabin Myth: A Study of the Early Dwellings of the English Colonists in North America* (Harvard University Press, 1939); C. A. Weslager, *The Log Cabin in America from Pioneer Days to the Present* (Rutgers University Press, 1969); and Terry G. Jordan and Matti Kaups, *The American Backwoods Frontier: An Ethnic and Ecological Interpretation* (Johns Hopkins University Press, 1989).

16. John T. Smith, "Concept of Diffusion," and "The Validity of Inference from Archaeological Evidence."

17. See, for example, Mercer, pp. 9, 10.

18. Slicher van Bath, p. 43.

19. Dyer, *Standards of Living,* pp. 79–80, and "English Peasant Buildings," pp. 28–29.

20. Slicher van Bath, pp. 42–43; and Horn and Born, *The Plan of St. Gall,* Vol. 1, pp. 344–345.

21. Slicher van Bath, p. 43.

22. Fergusson, pp. 166, 170, 172; R. Dohme, *Die Kirchen des Cistercienserordens in Deutschland während des Mittelalters* (Leipzig, 1869, pp. 34–35); Rösener, pp. 215, 216; and Aubert, Vol. 1, pp. 64, 98–99.

23. Bedal, personal communication.

24. Fred Kaspar, verbal communication.

25. Ellenberg.

Chapter 8

1. Herbert Bloch, p. 679.

2. See S. Bonde, R. Mark, and E. C. Robison, "Walls and Other Vertical Elements," in Mark, chapter 3; Widrig, *Ancient Roman Villa Gardens;* and Rossiter, p. 32, fig. 9, p. 44, fig. 13B, and p. 59.

3. Herbert Bloch, pp. 630–631.

4. Viollet-le-Duc, *Dictionnaire raisonné,* Vol. 3, "Charpente," pp. 1–58; and Courtenay, "Timber Roofs and Spires," pp. 189–191.

5. See Bans and Bans, "Continental Roofs"; and Meirion-Jones. For an opposite viewpoint, see Warren. While acknowledging that king-post roofs date back to the Roman occupation, the author argues they were not reintroduced until the Gothic period in response to the destructive effect of unrestrained tie-beams in timber roofs set above stone vaults.

6. See Courtenay, "Timber Roofs and Spires," pp. 206, 212; and John T. Smith, "Early Development of Timber Buildings." The *poinçons* in Warnavillers do not appear to be pegged to the tie-beams, which suggests that their role is not to support the beams but rather to counteract torque in the roof. Interestingly the *poinçons* in the nave trusses of the sixth-century monastery of St. Catherine at Mount Sinai do not even meet the tie-beams, indicating their function is to brace the principal rafters. See George H. Forsyth, *The Monastery of St. Catherine at Mount Sinai* (Ann Arbor, Michigan, 1973).

7. Viollet-le-Duc, *Dictionnaire raisonné,* Vol. 3, "Charpente," p. 11, fig. 7, and pp. 9–12. For an argument against any Roman influence in twelfth-century church roofs, see John T. Smith, "Mittelalterliche Dachkonstruktion." A twelfth-century date for Warnavillers was proposed by Dimier in "Les belles granges cisterciennes." In collaboration with Walter Horn, Rainer Berger in 1968 obtained a calibrated date of 931–1053 A.D. (Radiocarbon 28, 830, 1986) for the heartwood of an ashlar piece in the south wall of the barn. Veronika Siebenlist-Kerner took two further samples in 1969 but was unable to dendro-date them.

8. See Horn, "Great Tithe Barn of Cholsey," pp. 13–23, which also depicts details of the Canons' Barn at Wells; and Weller, *Canons' Barn.* Cholsey was demolished in the nineteenth century, and only a fragment of the Canons' Barn still exists.

9. Viollet-le-Duc, *Dictionnaire raisonné,* Vol. 3, "Charpente," pp. 35–36. See also Fletcher and Spokes; and Munby, Sparks, and Tatton-Brown.

10. Zimmermann, verbal communication; and Slofstra, pp. 143, 165. For a good illustration of pad stones used in the foundation of a third- to fifth-century aisled house from Gotland, Sweden, see Horn and Born, *The Plan of St. Gall,* Vol. 2, p. 37, fig. 291A.

11. See John Magilton, *The Archaeology of Chichester and District, 1990. Elsted: The Roman Villa Site at Batten Hanger [SU 818 153]* (Chichester District Council); and John T. Smith, "The Validity of Inference from Archaeological Evidence." For references to pad stones in other buildings of the Roman period in England, see Morris, p. 62.

12. Horn, "On the Origins of the Medieval Bay System," p. 16.

13. See Panofsky, who was alluding to church buildings rather than peasant housing.

14. For references other than Panofsky to a grammar of building construction, see John T. Smith, "The Validity of Inference from Archaeological Evidence," p. 13; Glassie, p. 229; echoed by Harris. For illustrations of the Palatine Chapel in Aachen and the Gatehouse at Lorsch, see Conant, plates 3 and 7; and Mark, pp. 98, 99.

15. Cassius Cocceianus Dio (Loeb Edition, Cambridge, Mass., 1914–1927, Vol. 6, Book LV. 8. 4); and Pliny the Elder, XVI. LXXVI. 201.

16. Boëthius and Ward-Perkins, p. 238; and Mark, pp. 54, 200–201.

17. Courtenay, "Timber Roofs and Spires," pp. 198–199.

18. See Rickman, *Roman Granaries*, pp. 236–241; Manning, "Roman Military Timber Granaries in Britain," and *The Fortress Excavations*; and Gentry.

19. Lynn T. Courtenay, "The Westminster Hall Roof and Its 14th-Century Sources" (*Journal of the Society of Architectural Historians*, Vol. 42, No. 4, 1984).

Chapter 9

1. Pliny the Elder, XVIII. LXXIII. 301–302.
2. See Gentry, p. 1.
3. Theophrastus, Vol. 1, Book V. VIII. 1–3.
4. Pliny the Elder, XVI. LXXVI. 200.
5. Meiggs, *Trees and Timber*, pp. 473–474.
6. Two splendid examples are the Palatine Chapel in Aachen and the Gatehouse at Lorsch, both late eighth century. See Mark, pp. 98, 99; and Conant, plates 3 and 7.
7. Gerda Panofsky-Soergel, *Abbot Suger on the Abbey Church of St. Denis and Its Art Treasures* (Princeton, New Jersey, 1979, pp. 95–97).
8. See Conant, p. 88; and Viollet-le-Duc, *Dictionnaire raisonné*, Vol. 1, "Architecture monastique," pp. 241–312. Odilo's comment seems to echo that of Augustus, who boasted that he had found Rome a city of mud-brick and left it a city of marble; see Meiggs, *Trees and Timber*, p. 238.
9. See Hewett, *English Historic Carpentry*; and D. D. Andrews. In Norway legend has it that prior to felling, the crowns were removed and the pines left standing for a couple of years to encourage resin to saturate the trunks and thus act as a preservative over the centuries. See Berg, *Norske Tømmerhus Frå Mellomalderen*, p. 268. According to Bruce Hoadley, professor of wood science at the University of Massachusetts, it is more likely that in the process the sapwood was replaced by more durable heartwood.
10. See Furrer. Konrad Bedal provided the information on surviving German buildings.
11. Max Gschwend and Benno Furrer, verbal communications. See also G. Bienz, "Wandlungen im Hausbau im alten Fürstbistum Basel, speziell im Delsberger Becken" (*Schweizer Volkskunde*, No. 6, Basel, 1952, pp. 86–92).
12. See Lerche.
13. See Rackham, *Ancient Woodland*, p. 7; and Kawashima, p. 17.
14. Rackham, *History of the Countryside*, pp. 75, 76, 88.
15. Dyer, "English Peasant Buildings," pp. 26–29; Mercer, pp. 27, 76, 105; and Addy, p. 234.
16. Rackham, *History of the Countryside*, pp. 86–87.
17. Cummings, pp. 50, 51.
18. Kalm, p. 300.
19. de Crèvecoeur, *Eighteenth-Century Travels*, p. 45.

Epilogue

1. Kidson, p. 71.

Appendix

1. For excellent accounts of Roman practices see Spurr; and White, *Roman Farming*.
2. Columella, Book II. XX. 4.
3. Diodorus of Sicily, III. V. 21.
4. Columella, Book II. XX. 2; and Pliny the Elder, V. LXXIII. 305. Spurr notes that the enlargement of the seed was established by controlled experiment. John Lacey of the Rothamsted Experimental Station in the U.K. believes the seed might actually be heavier before it is fully ripe, rather than growing in size after harvesting.
5. Columella, Book I. VI. 9 and I. VI. 15; John Lacey, "Storage of Barley Grain in Iron Age Type Underground Pits" (in *Journal of Stored Product Research*, Vol. 19, No. 4, Pergamon Press, 1983, pp. 163–171); Roymans, *Tribal Societies*, p. 106; and Pliny the Elder, V. LXXIII. 307.
6. Much of the following information concerning grain storage is based upon John Lacey, N. Ramakrishna, A. Hamer, N. Magan, and I. C. Marfleet, "Grain Fungi" (in *Handbook of Applied Mycology*, Vol. 3); N. Magan and J. Lacey, "Water and the Ecology of Grain Fungi" (in *Frontiers in Applied Microbiology*, Rastogi, India, Vol. 3, 1989); John Lacey, "Grain Storage: The Management of Ecological Change" (in *Biodeterioration* 7, D. R. Houghton, R. N. Smith, and H. O. W. Higgins, editors, Elsevier Applied Science, London); and John Lacey, "Pre- and Post-harvest Ecology of Fungi Causing Spoilage of Foods and Other Stored Products" (in *Journal of Applied Bacteriology Symposium Supplement*, 1989, pp. 11S-25S).
7. Gentry, p. 11.
8. See Iowa State University.
9. Columella, Book II. XX. 6; and White, *Roman Farming*, p. 187.
10. Columella, Book I. VI. 12–15.
11. Vitruvius, Book VI.VI. 4.
12. Pliny the Elder, V. LXXIII. 301 and 303.
13. Columella, Book II. XVIII. 1; and Vitruvius, VI.VI. 5.
14. Sir Francis Bacon, *Novum Organum* (trans. P. Shaw, 2 vols., London, 1802, pp. 186–187); and Charles A. Browne: *The Spontaneous Combustion of Hay* (U.S. Dept. of Agriculture, Bulletin No. 141, September 1929, p. 4).
15. See Pitt.
16. George Ewart Evans: *Ask the Fellows Who Cut the Hay* (U.K., 1956, p. 93); and Nigel Harvey, "'Riding the Goaf'—An Unusual Item of Barn Work" (in *Journal of the Historic Farm Buildings Group*, U.K., Vol. 5, 1991, pp. 3–8).

BIBLIOGRAPHY

Addy, Sidney O. *The Evolution of the English House* (4th edition, London, 1933).

Ahrens, Claus (editor). *Frühe Holzkirchen im Nördlichen Europa* (Hamburgisches Museum für Vor- und Frühgeschichte, 1981).

Altisent, Agusti. *Les Granges de Poblet al Segle XV: assaig d'història agrària d'unes granges cistercenques catalanes* (Institut d'Estudis Catalans, Premi Jaume Carner 1 Romeu, 1969, Barcelona 1972).

American Association of Cereal Chemists. *Storage of Cereal Grains and Their Products* (J. A. Anderson and A. W. Alcock, editors, St. Paul, Minnesota, 1954).

Andrews, D. D. (editor). *Cressing Temple: A Templar and Hospitaller Manor in Essex* (Essex County Council, 1993).

Andrews, F. B. *Mediaeval or "Tithe" Barns* (Transactions of the Proceedings of the Birmingham Archaeological Society, No. 26, 1900, pp. 10–32).

Arthur, Eric, and Dudley Witney. *The Barn: A Vanishing Landmark in North America* (New York Graphic Society, 1972).

Aubert, Marcel. *L'architecture cistercienne en France* (2 vols., Paris, 1947).

Bans, Jean-Christian, and Patricia Gaillard-Bans. "Continental Roofs: Some New Clues—Part 1" (*Vernacular Architecture*, No. 15, 1984, pp. 56–64).

———. "Hallenhäuser und Hallenscheunen in Frankreich" (*Jahrbuch für Hausforschung*, Vol. 34, 1984, pp. 151–181).

Barrière, Bernadette. "L'abbaye d'Obazine et ses granges" (in *Les Abbayes Cisterciennes et Leurs Granges*, Cahiers de la Ligue Urbaine et Rurale, No. 109, Paris, 1990, pp. 8–16).

———. "Le domaine cistercien" (in *Saint Bernard et Le Monde Cistercien*, Paris, CNMHS, 1990, pp. 94–111).

Baumeier, Stefan. *Westfälische Bauernhäuser Vor Bagger und Raupe gerettet* (Bielefeld, 1983).

Baumgarten, Karl. "Some Notes on the History of the German Hall House" (*Vernacular Architecture*, No. 7, 1976, pp. 15–20).

———. *Das deutsche Bauernhaus* (Berlin, 1980; reprinted Neumünster, 1985).

———. "Studies of Rural Buildings in Mecklenburg" (in *Technology and Culture*, Vol. 5, No. 2, Spring 1964, pp. 234–240).

Beacham, M. J. A. *West Country Tithe Barns* (Brewin Books, 1987).

———. *Midland Tithe Barns* (Brewin Books, 1989).

Bedal, Konrad. *Hallenhäuser und Längsscheunen des 18. und 19. Jahrhunderts im östlichen Holstein* (Neumünster, Wacholtz, 1980).

———. *Ländliche Ständerbauten des 15. bis 17. Jahrhunderts in Holstein und im südlichen Schleswig* (Neumünster, Wacholtz, 1977).

———. *Fachwerk vor 1600 in Franken: Eine Bestandsaufnahme* (Bad Windsheim, Fränkisches Freilandmuseum, 1990).

———. *Historische Hausforschung* (Coppenrath Verlag, 1978).

Beresford, Guy. *Goltho: The Development of an Early Medieval Manor c. 850–1150* (English Heritage, 1987).

Berg, Arne. *Norske Gardstun* (Oslo, 1968).

———. "Ein variant av Løa" (Saertrykk av *By Og Bygd*, Vol. 18, Oslo, 1966, pp. 137–142).

———. "Ei Løe Frå Mellomalderen" (Saertrykk av *By Og Bygd*, Vol. 19, Oslo, 1966, pp. 143–150).

———. "Korleis Bonden Bygde og Budde i Norrøn Tid" (Saerprent av *Årbok* for Telemark, 1973).

———. *Norske Tømmerhus Frå Mellomalderen, Vol. 1* (Oslo, 1989).

Berger, Rainer (editor). *Scientific Methods in Medieval Archaeology* (University of California Press, 1970).

Berman, Constance Hoffman. *Medieval Agriculture, the Southern French Countryside, and the Early Cistercians. A Study of Forty-three Monasteries* (Transactions of the American Philosophical Society, Philadelphia, Vol. 76, Part 5, 1986).

———. "Fortified Monastic Granges in the Rouergue" (in *The Medieval Castle: Romance and Reality*, Medieval Studies at Minnesota 1, Kathryn Reyerson and Faye Powe, editors, Iowa, 1984).

———. "Les granges cisterciennes fortifiées du Rouergue" (in *Les Abbayes Cisterciennes et Leurs Granges*, Cahiers de la Ligue Urbaine et Rurale, No. 109, Paris, 1990, pp. 54–65).

Biddle, M., and B. Clayre. *Winchester Castle and The Great Hall* (1983).

Binding, Günther. *Fachterminologie für den historischen Holzbau Fachwerk—Dachwerk* (Cologne, Abt. Architekturgeschichte des Kunsthistorischen Instituts, 1990).

———. *Das Dachwerk auf Kirchen im deutschen Sprachraum vom Mittelalter bis zum 18. Jahrhundert* (Munich, Deutscher Kunstverlag, 1991).

Blackburn, Roderic (editor). *New World Dutch Studies: Dutch Arts and Culture in Colonial America, 1609–1776* (Albany Institute of History and Art, 1987).

Blary, François. *Le Domaine de Chaalis XIIᵉ–XIVᵉ siècles: Approches archéologiques des établissements agricoles et industriels d'une abbaye cistercienne* (Paris, Éditions du C.T.H.S., 1989).

Bloch, Herbert. "The New Fascination with Ancient Rome" (in *Renaissance and Renewal in the Twelfth Century*, R. Benson and G. Constable, editors, Harvard University Press, 1982).

Bloch, Marc. *Feudal Society* (2 vols., London, Routledge & Kegan Paul, 1961).

———. *French Rural History* (London, 1966).

Bloemers, J. H. F. "Acculturation in the Rhine/Meuse Basin in the Roman Period: A Preliminary Survey" (in *Roman and Native in the Low Countries: Spheres of Interaction*, British Archaeological Review, International Series 184, 1983, pp. 159–204).

Boëthius, Axel, and J. B. Ward-Perkins. *Etruscan and Roman Architecture* (Harmondsworth, Pelican History of Art, Penguin Books, 1970).

Bonnet-Laborderie, Philippe, and Pierrette Bonnet-Laborderie. *Blé et Patrimoine: l'exemple cistercien* (Groupe d'Etude des Monuments et Oeuvres d'art du Beauvaisis, Bulletin No. 24, 1985).

Brandt, Roel, and Jan Slofstra (editors). *Roman and Native in the Low Countries: Spheres of Interaction* (British Archaeological Review, International Series 184, 1983).

Braunfels, Wolfgang. *Monasteries of Western Europe: The Architecture of the Orders* (London, Thames & Hudson, 1972).

Cahiers de la Ligue Urbaine et Rurale. *Les Abbayes Cisterciennes et Leurs Granges* (Patrimoine et Cadre de Vie, No. 109, Paris, 1990).

Cambridge Economic History of Europe. *The Agrarian Life of the Middle Ages* (Vol. 1, 2nd edition, M. M. Postan, editor, Cambridge University Press, 1966).

Carter, H. Malcolm. *The Fort of Othona and the Chapel of St. Peter-on-the-Wall, Bradwell-on-Sea, Essex* (St. Peter's Chapel Committee, 1987).

Cato and Varro. *On Agriculture* (Trans. W. D. Hooper, Loeb Library, 1934).

Centre Culturel de l'Abbaye de Flaran. *L'Économie Cistercienne: Géographie—Mutations du Moyen Age aux Temps modernes* (Auch, 1983).

Chouquer, Gérard, and Hans de Klijn. "Le Finage Antique et Médiéval" (in *Gallia*, Paris, Vol. 46, 1989, pp. 261–299).

Clough, T. H. McK. (editor). *Oakham Castle, a Guide and History* (Rutland, 1987).

Cohen, David Steven. "Dutch-American Farming: Crops, Livestock, and Equipment, 1623–1900" (in *New World Dutch Studies: Dutch Arts and Culture in Colonial America, 1609–1776*, Roderic Blackburn, editor, Albany, 1987, pp. 185–200).

———. *The Dutch-American Farm* (New York University Press, 1992).

———. "How Dutch Were the Dutch of New Netherland?" (*New York History*, January 1981, pp. 43–60).

Columella, Lucius Junius Moderatus. *On Agriculture* (with a recension of the text and an English translation by Harrison Boyd Ash, 3 vols., Harvard University Press, Loeb Classical Library, 1941–1955).

Comeaux, Malcolm L. "The Cajun Barn" (in *Geographical Review*, Vol. 79, No. 1, 1989, pp. 47–62).

Conant, Kenneth John. *Carolingian and Romanesque Architecture 800–1200* (Penguin Books, 1959).

Constable, Giles. *Monastic Tithes from Their Origins to the Twelfth Century* (Cambridge University Press, 1964).

Cooter, W. S. "Ecological Dimensions of Medieval Agrarian Systems" (in *Agricultural History*, Vol. 52, No. 4, 1978, pp. 458–477).

Coppack, Glyn. "The Excavation of an Outer Court Building, Perhaps the Woolhouse, at Fountains Abbey, North Yorkshire" (in *Medieval Archaeology*, Vol. 30, 1986, pp. 46–87).

Courtenay, Lynn T. "Timber Roofs and Spires" (in *Architectural Technology up to the Scientific Revolution*, Robert Mark, editor, MIT Press, 1993, pp. 182–231).

Courtenay, Lynn T., and R. Mark. *Parçay-Meslay (Indre-et-Loire) France, 9 km. Northeast of Tours* (Unpublished manuscript, circa 1987/88, in the Walter Horn/Ernest Born Archives No. 920089, Resource Collections of the Getty Center for the History of Art and the Humanities, Santa Monica, California).

Cummings, Abbott Lowell. *The Framed Houses of Massachusetts Bay, 1625–1725* (Harvard University Press, 1979).

Danckaerts, Jasper. *Journal of Jasper Danckaerts, 1679–1680* (New York, Charles Scribner, 1913).

D'Arbois de Jubainville, Marie Henri. *Études sur l'état intérieur des abbayes Cisterciennes, et principalement de Clairvaux au XIIe et au XIIIe siècle* (Paris, 1858).

David Roy, Marguerite. "Les granges monastiques en France aux XIIe et XIIIe siècles" (in *Archéologia*, No. 58, 1973, pp. 52–62).

de Crèvecoeur, Michel-Guillaume St. Jean. *Eighteenth-Century Travels in Pennsylvania and New York* (University of Kentucky Press, 1961).

———. *Sketches of Eighteenth-Century America: More "Letters from an American Farmer"* (New Haven, Yale University Press, 1925).

Deneux, H. *Charpentes: L'Evolution des Charpentes du XIe au XVIIIe siècles* (Centre de recherches sur les Monuments Historiques, 1961).

Dimier, Père Anselme. "Granges, celliers et bâtiments d'exploitation cisterciens" (in *Archéologia*, No. 65, 1973, pp. 52–63).

———. "Les belles granges cisterciennes de l'Oise" (in *Archéologia*, No. 85, 1975, pp. 49–61).

Dopsch, Alfons. "Agrarian Institutions of the Germanic Kingdoms from the Fifth to the Ninth Century" (in Cambridge Economic History of Europe, *The Agrarian Life of the Middle Ages*, Vol. 1, 2nd edition, M. M. Postan, editor, Cambridge University Press, 1966, pp. 180–204).

Drack, Walter. "Die Gutshöfe" (in *Ur- und frühgeschichtlich Archäologie der Schweiz 5. Die römische Epoche*, Basel, 1975, pp. 49–72).

Dubois, P. "Les granges d'abbaye aux XIe et XIIe siècles en Picardie et en Flandre" (in *Bulletin de la Societé des Antiquaires en Picardie*, 1907–1908, pp. 564–565).

Duby, Georges. *Rural Economy and Country Life in the Medieval West* (Trans. Cynthia Postan, Edward Arnold, 1968).

Durand, Robert. "L'économie cistercienne au Portugal" (in Centre Culturel de l'Abbaye de Flaran, *L'Économie Cistercienne: Géographie—Mutations du Moyen Age aux Temps modernes*, Auch, 1983, pp. 101–117).

Dyer, Christopher. "English Peasant Buildings in the Later Middle Ages" (in *Medieval Archaeology*, Vol. 30, 1986, pp. 19–45).

———. *Standards of Living in the Later Middle Ages: Social Change in England c. 1200–1520* (Cambridge University Press, 1989).

Einhard and Notker the Stammerer. *Two Lives of Charlemagne* (Trans. Lewis Thorpe, London, Penguin Books, 1969).

Eitzen, Gerhard. *Niederrheinische Bauernhäuser vom 15. bis zum Beginn des 18. Jahrhunderts* (Führer und Schriften des Rheinischen Freilichtmuseums und Landesmuseums für Volkskunde in Kommern, No. 19, Cologne, 1987).

———. *Bauernhäuser aus Mitteleuropa: Aufmasse und Publikationen* (Sobernheim/Bad Windsheim, 1984).

Ellenberg, Heinz. *Bauernhaus und Landschaft in ökologischer und historischer Sicht* (Stuttgart, 1990).

Engqvist, Hans Henrik. "Jyske og fynske herregårdslader" (in *Bygnings Arkaeologiske Studier 87*, Copenhagen, 1987, pp. 7–32).

Fergusson, Peter. *Architecture of Solitude: Cistercian Abbeys in Twelfth-Century England* (Princeton, 1984).

Fitchen, John. *The New World Dutch Barn. A Study of Its Characteristics, Its Structural System, and Its Probable Erectional Procedures* (Syracuse, 1968).

Fletcher, J. M., and P. S. Spokes. "The Origin and Development of Crown-post Roofs" (in *Medieval Archaeology*, Vol. 8, 1964, pp. 152–183).

Flores, Carlos. *Arquitectura Popular Española* (5 vols., Madrid, Aguilar, 1973).

Fokkens, Harry, and Nico Roymans, editors. *Nederlandse Archeologische Rapporten, No. 13* (Rijksdienst voor het Oudheidkundig Bodemonderzoek, Amersfoort, 1991).

Fournee, Dr. J. *Abbaye Notre-Dame d'Ardenne [Calvados]* (Annee des Abbayes Normandes, No. 10, 1979).

Fowler, Rev. Canon T. "Further Notes on Clairvaux, and a Note on Cîteaux" (in *Yorkshire Archaeological Journal*, Vol. 20, 1909).

Frayn, Joan M. *Subsistence Farming in Roman Italy* (London, Centaur Press, 1979).

Furrer, Benno. "Beiträge zur Hausgeschichte des 13. und 14. Jahrhunderts in der Innerschweiz" (in *Der Geschichtsfreund*, Stans, Vol. 141, 1988, pp. 175–200).

Fussell, G. E. *The Classical Tradition in West European Farming* (U.K., David & Charles, 1972).

Ganshof, F. L. *Feudalism* (London, 1959).

———. "Manorial Organization in the Low Countries in the Seventh, Eighth and Ninth Centuries" (in *Transactions of the Royal Historical Society*, 4th Series, Vol. 31, 1949, pp. 29–59).

Ganshof, F. L., and A. Verhulst. "Medieval Agrarian Society in Its Prime: France, the Low Countries, and Western Germany" (in Cambridge Economic History of Europe, *The Agrarian Life of the Middle Ages*, Vol. 1, 2nd edition, M. M. Postan, editor, Cambridge University Press, 1966, pp. 291–339).

Garnsey, Peter. *Famine and Food Supply in the Graeco-Roman World; Responses to Risk and Crisis* (Cambridge University Press, 1988).

Gehring, Charles T. "Material Culture in Seventeenth-Century Dutch Colonial

Manuscripts" (in *New World Dutch Studies: Dutch Arts and Culture in Colonial America, 1609–1776*, Roderic Blackburn, editor, Albany, 1987, pp. 43–49).

Gem, Richard. "Church Architecture" (in *The Making of England: Anglo-Saxon Art and Culture*, A.D. 600–900, British Museum Press, 1991, pp. 185–188).

Gentry, Anne P. "Roman Military Stone-built Granaries in Britain (in *British Archaeological Review* 32, 1976).

Gjaerder, Per. *Vest-Norske Utløer i Stav-Verk* (Oslo, 1977).

Glassie, Henry. "The Variation of Concepts Within Tradition: Barn Building in Otsego County, New York" (in *Geoscience and Man,* Vol. 5, *Man and Cultural Heritage,* Louisiana State University, 1974).

Gottfried, Robert S. *The Black Death: Natural and Human Disaster in Medieval Europe* (New York, Macmillan, 1983).

Grant, Mrs. Anne. *Memoirs of an American Lady: With Sketches of Manners and Scenes in America as They Existed Previous to the Revolution* (New York, Dodd, Mead, 1901).

Graves, Coburn V. "Medieval Cistercian Granges" (in *Studies in Medieval Culture, Vol. 2,* J. R. Sommerfeldt, editor, Kalamazoo, Michigan, 1966, pp. 63–70).

Gregory of Tours. *The History of the Franks* (Trans. Lewis Thorpe, London, Penguin Books, 1974).

Gröenman van Wateringe, W. "The Disastrous Effect of the Roman Occupation" (in *Roman and Native in the Low Countries: Spheres of Interaction,* British Archaeological Review, International Series 184, 1983).

Hagens, H. *Schuren in Twente* (Rijksmuseum, Enschede, 1983. Manuscript).

————. *Boerderijen in Twente* (Utrecht, Uitgeverij Matrijs, 1992).

Halbout, Patrick, and Jacques Le Maho. *Aspects de la construction de bois en Normandie* (Caen, Centre Archéologique de Normandie, 1984).

Harris, Richard. "The Grammar of Carpentry" (in *Vernacular Architecture,* No. 20, 1989, pp. 1–8).

Harsema, O. H. "Structural Reconstruction of Iron Age Houses in the Northern Netherlands" (in *Structural Reconstruction: Approaches to the Interpretation of the Excavated Remains of Buildings,* British Archaeological Review, British Series 110, 1982, pp. 199–222).

Hartshorne, Albert. *The Great Barn, Harmondsworth* (Transactions of the London and Middlesex Archaeological Society).

Heidinga, H. A. *Medieval Settlement and Economy North of the Lower Rhine* (Maastricht, 1987).

Hekker, R. C. *Duizend Jaar Bouwen in Nederland* (Amsterdam, Allert de Lange, 1957).

————. *Historische Boerderijtypen/Historical Types of Farms* (Arnhem, SHBO, 1991).

————. "Farmstead Villages in the Netherlands" (in *Vernacular Architecture,* No. 4, 1973, pp. 7–12).

Helm, Rudolf. *Das Bauernhaus im Alt-Nürnberger Gebeit* (reprint, Nuremberg, 1978).

Herman, Bernard L. *Architecture and Rural Life in Central Delaware 1700–1900* (University of Tennessee Press, 1987).

Hessing, Wilfried. "Bewoningssporen uit de midden-bronstijd en de vroege ijzertijd op 'De Horden' te Wijk bij Duurstede" (in *Nederlandse Archeologische Rapporten, No. 13,* Fokkens and Roymans, editors, Amersfoort, Rijksdienst voor het Oudheidkundig Bodemonderzoek, 1991).

Hewett, Cecil A. *English Historic Carpentry* (Phillimore, 1980).

————. *English Cathedral and Monastic Carpentry* (Phillimore, 1985).

————. "The Barns at Cressing Temple, Essex, and Their Significance in the History of English Carpentry" (in *Journal of the Society of Architectural Historians,* Vol. 26, No. 1, March 1967).

Higounet, Charles. *La Grange de Vaulerent: Structure et exploitation d'un terroir cistercien de la plaine de France, XIIe–XVe siècle* (Les hommes et la terre, 10: Paris, S.E.V.P.E.N., 1965).

————. "Essai sur les granges cisterciennes" (in Centre Culturel de l'Abbaye de Flaran, *L'Économie Cistercienne: Géographie—Mutations du Moyen Age aux Temps modernes,* Auch, 1983, pp. 157–180).

Hinz, Hermann. "Einfahrtstor und Erntebergung. Gedanken zum Stammbaum der niederdeutschen Halle [Niedersachsenhaus]" (in *Bonner Jahrbucher des Rheinischen Landesmuseums in Bonn,* No. 158, 1958, pp. 118–125).

————. "Zur Vorgeschichte der Niederdeutschen Halle" (in *Zeitschrift für Volkskunde,* 60, Jahrgang, 1964, pp. 1–22).

————. "Zur Entwicklung der Niederdeutschen Halle [Niedersachsenhaus]" (in *Sonderdruck aus Nordelbingen,* Vol. 23, pp. 17–22).

————. *Ländlicher Hausbau in Skandinavien vom 6. bis 14. Jahrhundert: Stova-Eldhus-Bur* (Cologne, Rheinland-Verlag, 1989).

Hole, Frank. "Middle Khabur Settlement and Agriculture in the Ninevite 5 Period" (in *Bulletin of the Canadian Society for Mesopotamian Studies,* No. 21, Toronto, 1991, pp. 17–29).

Horn, Walter. "On the Origins of the Medieval Bay System" (in *Journal of the Society of Architectural Historians,* Vol. 17, No. 2, Summer 1958).

———. "On the Origins of the Medieval Cloister" (in *Gesta,* Vol. 12, 1973, pp. 13–52).

———. "The Great Tithe Barn of Cholsey, Berkshire" (in *Journal of the Society of Architectural Historians,* Vol. 22, No. 1, March 1963).

———. "Survival, Revival, Transformation: The Dialectic of Development in Architecture and Other Arts" (in *Renaissance and Renewal in the Twelfth Century,* R. Benson and G. Constable, editors, Harvard University Press, 1982).

Horn, Walter, and Ernest Born. *The Plan of St. Gall* (3 vols., University of California Press, 1979).

———. *The Barns of the Abbey of Beaulieu at Its Granges of Great Coxwell and Beaulieu-St. Leonards* (University of California Press, 1965).

———. "Buildings in the Domesday of St. Paul's Cathedral" (in *Saints, Scholars and Heroes: Studies in Medieval Culture,* Vol. 2, Minnesota, 1979, pp. 343–417).

———. *The Barn of the Cistercian Grange of Vaulerent (Seine-et-Oise), France* (Berlin, 1968).

———. "French Market Halls in Timber: Medieval and Postmedieval" (in *The Shape of the Past: Studies in Honor of Franklin D. Murphy,* G. Buccellati and C. Speroni, editors, Los Angeles, 1981, pp. 195–239).

———. "Les Halles de Crémieu" (in *Bulletin du Groupe d'Etudes Historiques et Géographiques du Bas Dauphiné,* No. 3, 1961, pp. 66–90).

———. "Water Power and the Plan of St. Gall" (in *Journal of Medieval History 1,* 1975, pp. 219–258).

Horn, Walter, and F. W. B. Charles. "The Cruck-built Barn of Leigh Court, Worcestershire, England" (in *Journal of the Society of Architectural Historians,* Vol. 32, No. 1, March 1973).

Hubka, Thomas C. *Big House, Little House, Back House, Barn: The Connected Farm Buildings of New England* (University Press of New England, 1984).

Huijts, C. S. T. J. *De voor-historische boerderijbouw in Drenthe. Reconstructiemodellen van 1300 vóór tot 1300 na Chr.* (Arnhem, SHBO, 1992).

Hutton, Barbara. "Aisles to Outshots" (in *Archaeological Papers from York,* York, 1984).

Iowa State University. *Grain Drying, Handling and Storage Handbook* (2nd edition, Midwest Plan Service, 1988).

Ispir, Mihai. "Ratoşele din Moldova" (in *Revista Muzeelor si Monumentelor: Monumente Istorice si de Arta, No. 1,* Bucharest, 1976).

James, Simon, Anne Marshall, and Martin Millet. "An Early Medieval Building Tradition" (in *Archaeological Journal,* Vol. 141, 1984).

Jameson, J. Franklin (editor). *Narratives of New Netherland, 1607–1664* (New York, Charles Scribner, 1909).

Jans, Jan. *Landelijke in Oost-Nederland* (Enschede, 1967).

Janse, H. *Bouwtechniek in Nederland 2. Houten kappen in Nederland, 1000–1940* (Delftse Universitaire Pers, Rijksdienst voor de Monumentenzorg, 1989).

———. "Trusses with Curved Principals in Western Europe" (in *Vernacular Architecture,* No. 11, 1980, pp. 12–16).

———. "De Abdijschuur van Ter Doest" (in *Bulletin K.N.O.B. 6de serie 17,* 1964, pp. 189–202).

Janse, H., and L. Devliegher. "Middeleeuwse bekappingen in hey vroegere graafschap Vlanderen" (in *Bulletin Kon. Commissie Monumenten en Landschappen 13,* Brussels, 1982).

Jones, Charles W. "The Customs of Corbie" (in Horn and Born, *The Plan of St. Gall,* Vol. 3, University of California Press, 1979, Appendix II, p. 112 and following).

Jones, Stanley R. "Gunthwaite Hall Barn" (in *Archaeological Journal,* Vol. 137, 1980, pp. 463–466).

Kalm, Peter. *Peter Kalm's Travels in North America: The English Version of 1770* (reprint, New York, Dover, 1987).

Katz, Solomon H., and Mary M Voigt. "Bread and Beer: The Early Use of Cereals in the Human Diet" (in *Expedition,* Journal of the University Museum, Philadelphia, Vol. 28, No. 2, 1986, pp. 23–34).

Kawashima, Chuji. *Minka: Traditional Houses of Rural Japan* (Tokyo, Kodansha, 1986).

Kidson, Peter. "A Metrological Investigation" (in *Journal of the Warburg and Courtauld Institutes,* Vol. 53, 1990, pp. 71–97).

Kinder, Terryl N. "L'abbaye cistercienne" (in *Saint Bernard et Le Monde Cistercien,* Paris, CNMHS, 1990, pp. 77–93).

———. "Les granges de l'abbaye de Pontigny" (in *Les Abbayes Cisterciennes et Leurs Granges,* Cahiers de la Ligue Urbaine et Rurale, No. 109, Paris, 1990, pp. 33–39).

Kniffen, Fred B. "Folk Housing: Key to Diffusion" (in *Common Places,* University of Georgia Press, 1986).

Koebner, Richard. "The Settlement and Colonization of Europe" (in Cambridge Economic History of Europe, *The Agrarian Life of the Middle Ages,* Vol. 1, 2nd edition, M. M. Postan, editor, Cambridge University Press, 1966, pp. 1–91).

Krautheimer, Richard. *Early Christian and Byzantine Architecture* (Penguin Books, 1965).

LaChapelle, Jack. *"Halle et Grange"* (Unpublished paper in the Walter Horn/Ernest Born Archives No. 920089, Resource Collections of the Getty Center for the History of Art and the Humanities, Santa Monica, California).

Lamond, Elizabeth. *Walter of Henley's Husbandry, Together with an Anonymous Husbandry, Seneschaucie and Robert Grosseteste's Rules* (London, Longmans, 1890).

Larson, Neil. "New York's Dutch Barns: A Functional Perspective" (in *Pioneer American Society Transactions,* Vol. 10, 1987, pp. 37–41).

Lassure, Christian. "A propos des 'maisons-halle' du Berry: La 'maison carree' de Villegenon, commune de Vailly-sur-Sauldre [Cher]" (in *L'Architecture Vernaculaire,* Vol. 5, 1981, pp. 33–34).

———. "Une 'maison-halle' a Montcaret [Dordogne]" (in *L'Architecture Vernaculaire,* Vol. 5, 1981, pp. 35–36).

———. "A propos des 'maisons-halle' du Berry: un rare temoin a Saint-Phalier, commune de Levroux [Indre]" (in *L'Architecture Vernaculaire,* Vol. 5, 1981, pp. 57–58).

———. "Les 'maisons-halle' en Saintonge et en Angoumois a la lumiere de releves anciens et recents" (in *L'Architecture Vernaculaire,* Vol. 6, 1982, pp. 34–40).

———. "La tradition supra-regionale des maisons-halle en Lorraine: un accroc au mythe regionaliste de 'la maison rurale de type Lorrain'" (in *L'Architecture Vernaculaire,* Vol. 7, 1983, pp. 39–51).

———. "Une grange a dimes du XVIᵉ siècle (?) a Poncey-sur-L'Ignon [Cote-d'Or]" (in *L'Architecture Vernaculaire,* Vol. 12, 1988, pp. 27–47).

———. "Sur quelques constructions a Pauxfourches, balanciers de puits et batiments de type halle dans le nord-est de la Dordogne" (in *L'Architecture Vernaculaire,* Vol. 13, 1989, pp. 81–86).

———. "La grange a dimes de Chauzanaud a Savignac-les-Eglises (Dordogne): stude architecturale d'une grange a nef et bas-cotes du XVIIᵉ siècle" (in *L'Architecture Vernaculaire,* Vol. 14, 1990, pp. 61–68).

Lassure, Christian, and Benoît Delaroziére. "Une 'maison-halle' des XVIᵉ–XVIIᵉ siècles (?) a Saint-Jean-de Bonneval [Aube]" (in *L'Architecture Vernaculaire,* Vol. 5, 1981, pp. 21–32).

Lassure, Christian, and Jean-Michel Lassure. "Les maisons rurales du Gers aux XVIIIᵉ et XIXᵉ siècles: modeles bourgeois et modeles paysans" (in *L'Architecture Vernaculaire,* Vol. 5, 1981, pp. 46–51).

Leblanc, M. G. "La Grange Lassale: Etude historique et archéologique d'une 'grange' cistercienne" (in *Actes de la Congrès des Sociétés Savantes,* Montarbon, 1954, pp. 3–16).

———. *La Grange Cistercienne de Fontcalvi [Aude]* (XXXᵐᵉ Congrès-Séte).

Le Goff, Jacques. *Medieval Civilization* (English translation, Oxford, 1988).

Lekai, Louis J. *The White Monks: A History of the Cistercian Order* (Wisconsin, Okauchee, 1953).

Lemaitre, Mme Philippe. "Note sur quelques granges dimiéres du Département de l'Eure" (in *Bulletin Monumental,* 1849, pp. 193–198).

Lenoir, Albert. *Architecture Monastique* (2 vols., Paris, 1852–1856).

Lepper, Frank, and Sheppard Frere. *Trajan's Column: A New Edition of the Cichorius Plates* (Gloucester, Alan Sutton, 1988).

Lerche, Grith. "Timber-framed Buildings in Denmark" (in *Vernacular Architecture,* No. 4, 1973).

Leroux, Jean-François. "Les granges et celliers de Clairvaux" (in *Les Abbayes Cisterciennes et Leurs Granges,* Cahiers de la Ligue Urbaine et Rurale, No. 109, Paris, 1990, pp. 17–23).

Leroy, A., and P. A. Wimet. "La grange cistercienne de la Longueroye" (in *Bulletin de la Commission Départementale des Monuments Historiques du Pas-de-Calais,* Vol. 9, No. 2, 1972, pp. 154–163).

Le Roy Ladurie, Emmanuel. *Times of Feast, Times of Famine: A History of Climate Since the Year 1000* (English translation, New York, 1988).

Lescroart-Cazenave, Élizabeth. "Les granges médiévales" (in *Le Prieuré Saint-Michel de Crouttes,* Monuments Historiques).

Lindner, Werner. *Das niedersächsische Bauernhaus in Deutschland und Holland* (Hannover, 1912; reprinted 1987).

Manning, W. H. "Roman Military Timber Granaries in Britain" (in *Sallburg Jahrbuch,* 32, Berlin, 1975, pp. 105–129).

———. *The Fortress Excavations 1968–1971* (Report on the excavations at Usk 1965–1976, Cardiff, University of Wales Press, 1981).

Mark, Robert (editor). *Architectural Technology up to the Scientific Revolution* (MIT Press, 1993).

Martin, David, and Barbara Martin. *Historic Buildings in Eastern Sussex,* Vol. 1 (Rape of Hastings Architectural Survey, 1977–1980).

———. *Historic Buildings in Eastern Sussex,* Vol. 3, *Old Farm Buildings in Eastern Sussex, 1450–1750* (Rape of Hastings Architectural Survey, 1982).

Maschmeyer, Dietrich. "Detaillierte Hausforschung in einem kleinen Gebiet—Methodik und Ziele der Forschung in der Grafschaft Bentheim" (in *Hausbau in Münster und Westfalen,* Jahrbuch für Hausforschung 36/37, Sobernheim, 1987, pp. 249–279).

McVeigh, S. A. J. *Harmondsworth's Glory* (Unpublished paper, 1979).

Meiggs, Russell. *Roman Ostia* (Oxford University Press, 1973).

———. *Trees and Timber in the Ancient Mediterranean World* (Oxford University Press, 1982).

Meirion-Jones, Gwyn I. "The Vernacular Architecture of France: An Assessment" (in *Vernacular Architecture,* No. 16, 1985, pp. 1–24).

Mercer, Eric. *English Vernacular Houses* (RCHM, 1975; paperback reprint 1979).

Miller, Edward, and John Hatcher. *Medieval England: Rural Society and Economic Change, 1086–1348* (London, 1978).

Millet, Martin, with Simon James. "Excavations at Cowdery's Down, Basingstoke, Hampshire, 1978–81" (in *Archaeological Journal,* Vol. 140, 1983).

Ministère des Affaires Culturelles. Inventaire Général des Monuments et des Richesses Artistiques de la France. Commission Régionale d'Aquitaine. *Landes: canton Peyrehorade* (2 vols., Paris, 1973).

Ministère de la Culture, Centre de Recherches sur les Monuments Historiques. *Charpentes, Vol. I, XIe–XIIe Siècles* (Paris, 1982).

———. *Charpentes de halles et de granges, Vol. I, XVe et XVIe Siècles, Régions diverses* (Paris, 1983).

Morehart, Mary. *Iconograph of the Cistercian Abbey of Clairvaux* (Unpublished manuscript, dated spring 1950, in the Walter Horn/Ernest Born Archives No. 920089, Resource Collections of the Getty Center for the History of Art and the Humanities, Santa Monica, California).

Morris, Pat. "Agricultural Buildings in Roman Britain" (in *British Archaeological Review,* British Series 70, 1979).

Multon, J. L. (editor). *Preservation and Storage of Grains, Seeds and Their By-Products* (Paris and New York, Lavoisier).

Munby, Julian. "Great Coxwell Barn" (in *Archaeological Journal,* Supplement to Vol. 145, 1988).

Munby, J., M. Sparks, and T. Tatton-Brown. "Crown-post and King-strut Roofs in South-East England" (in *Medieval Archaeology,* Vol. 27, 1983, pp. 123–135).

Musset, L. *Prieuré de Perrières [Calvados]* (Annee des Abbayes Normandes, No. 2).

Musso, J.-M., and M. Miguet. "Le bâtiment des convers de l'abbaye de Clair-vaux, Histoire, archéologie, restauration" (in *Les Abbayes Cisterciennes et Leurs Granges,* Cahiers de la Ligue Urbaine et Rurale, No. 109, Paris, 1990, pp. 24–32).

Noble, Allen G. *Wood, Brick and Stone: The North American Settlement Landscape* (University of Massachusetts Press, 1984).

Offa. *Berichte und Mitteilungen zur Urgeschichte, Frühgeschichte und Mittelalterarchäologie,* Vol. 39, 1982 (Neumünster, Carl Wacholtz Verlag, 1982).

Ostendorf, Friedrich. *Die Geschichte des Dachwerks* (Leipzig, 1908; reprinted Hannover, 1982).

Oswald, F., L. Schaeffer, and H. R. Sennhauser. *Vorromanische Kirchenbauten* (2 vols., Munich, Prestel Verlag, 1990).

Panofsky, Erwin. *Gothic Architecture and Scholasticism* (New American Library, 1976).

Parain, Charles. "The Evolution of Agricultural Technique" (in Cambridge Economic History of Europe, *The Agrarian Life of the Middle Ages,* Vol. 1, 2nd edition, M. M. Postan, editor, Cambridge University Press, 1966, pp. 125–179).

Parker, John Henry. *Some Account of Domestic Architecture in England from Edward I to Richard II* (1st edition, Oxford, 1853).

Parker, John Henry, and James Parker. *Some Account of Domestic Architecture in England from Richard II to Henry VIII* (Parts I and II, Oxford, 1859).

Parkman, Francis. *France and England in North America,* Vol. 1 (New York, 1983).

Percival, John. *The Roman Villa: An Historical Introduction* (London, Batsford, 1976; reprinted 1988).

Perez-Embid Wamba, J. *El Cister en Castilla y León. Monacata y dominios rurales [siglos XII–XV]* (Salamanca, 1986).

Pitt, R. E. *Silage and Hay Preservation* (Northeast Regional Agricultural Engineering Service, Ithaca, New York, 1990).

Platt, Colin. *The Monastic Grange in Medieval England* (London, Macmillan, 1969).

Pliny the Elder. *Natural History* (Trans. H. Rackham, Loeb Library, 1960).

Portela Silva, Ermelindo. *La colonizacion Cisterciense en Galicia, 1142–1250* (Universidad de Santiago de Compostela, 1981).

Postan, M. M. *The Medieval Economy and Society* (Penguin Books, 1972).

Précheur-Canonge, Thérèse. *La vie rurale en Afrique romaine d'après les mosaïques* (Presses Universitaires de France, 1962).

Pressouyre, Léon, *Le rêve cistercien* (Paris, CNMHS, 1990).

Pressouyre, Léon and Terryl Kinder. *Saint Bernard et Le Monde Cistercien* (Paris, CNMHS, 1990).

Rackham, Oliver. *Ancient Woodland: Its History, Vegetation and Uses in England* (London, Edward Arnold, 1980).

———. *Trees and Woodland in the British Landscape* (revised edition, London, J. M. Dent, 1990).

Radford, C. A. R. "Oakham Castle" (in *Archaeological Journal,* Vol. 112, 1955, pp. 181–184).

Rahtz, Philip. "The Saxon and Medieval Palaces at Cheddar, Somerset—An Interim Report of Excavations in 1960–62" (in *Medieval Archaeology,* Vols. 6–7, 1962–1963, pp. 53–66).

Rahtz, P., J. T. Smith, Guy Beresford, and P. A. Barker. "Architectural Reconstruction of Timber Buildings from Archaeological Evidence" (in *Vernacular Architecture,* No. 13, 1982, pp. 39–47).

Reed, Carl. "Development of Storage Techniques: A Historical Perspective" (in *Storage of Cereal Grains and Their Products,* American Association of Cereal Chemists, St. Paul, Minnesota, 1992).

Reynolds, Peter. *Ancient Farming* (Shire Publications, 1987).

———. "Slash and Burn Experiment" (in *Archaeological Journal,* Vol. 134, 1977, pp. 307–318).

Reynolds, P. J., and J. K. Langley. "Romano-British Corn-Drying Oven: An Experiment" (in *Archaeological Journal,* Vol. 136, 1979, pp. 27–42).

Rickman, Geoffrey. *Roman Granaries and Store Buildings* (Cambridge University Press, 1971).

———. *The Corn Supply of Ancient Rome* (Oxford University Press, 1980).

Rigold, S. E. "Some Major Kentish Barns" (in *Archaeologia Cantiana,* Vol. 81, 1966, pp. 1–30).

———. "The Distribution of Aisled Timber Barns" (in *Vernacular Architecture,* No. 2, 1971, pp. 20–21).

Rochon, Bernard. "Les granges médiévales: de la fonction à l'abandon" (in *Les Abbayes Cisterciennes et Leurs Granges,* Cahiers de la Ligue Urbaine et Rurale, No. 109, Paris, 1990, pp. 52–53).

Rodriguez, Ignacio Martinez. *El hòrreo gallego* (Fundacion Pedro Barrié de la Maza, Conde de Fenosa, La Coruña, 1979).

Rösener, Werner. *Peasants in the Middle Ages* (Cambridge, Polity Press, 1992).

Rossiter, J. J. "Roman Farm Buildings in Italy" (in *British Archaeological Review,* International Series 52, 1978).

Roymans, Nico. *Tribal Societies in Northern Gaul: An Anthropological Perspective* (Universiteit van Amsterdam, Instituut voor Pre- en Protohistorische Archeologie Albert Egges van Giffen, Cingula 12, Amsterdam, 1990).

Roymans, Nico, and Frans Theuws (editors). *Images of the Past: Studies on Ancient Societies in North-western Europe* (Instituut voor Pre- en Protohistorische Archeologie Albert Egges van Giffen, Amsterdam, 1991).

Schepers, Josef. *Haus und Hof westfälischer Bauern* (Münster, Aschendorff, 1977).

———. *Der Lippische Meierhof im Westfälischen Freilichtmuseum Detmold* (Detmold, 1982).

———. *Das Bauernhaus in Nordwestdeutschland* (Bielefeld, Küster Pressedruck, 1978).

Schwartz, Glenn M. "The Ninevite V Period and the Development of Complex Society in Northern Mesopotamia" (in *Paléorient,* Vol. 13/2, pp. 93–100).

Schwartz, Glenn M., and Hans H. Curvers. "Tell al-Raqā'i 1989 and 1990: Further Investigations at a Small Rural Site of Early Urban Northern Mesopotamia" (in *American Journal of Archaeology,* July 1992, pp. 397–419).

Schweizer Baudokumentation. "Maisons rurales dans le Hau-Jura" (Schweizer Baukatalog, 1968, Code AXZ 110).

Slicher van Bath, B. H. *The Agrarian History of Western Europe,* A.D. 500–1850 (Edward Arnold, 1963).

Slofstra, Jan. "Changing Settlement Systems in the Meuse-Demer-Scheldt Area during the Early Roman Period" (in *Images of the Past: Studies on Ancient Societies in North-western Europe,* Nico Roymans and Frans Theuws, editors, Instituut voor Pre- en Protohistorische Archeologie Albert Egges van Giffen, Amsterdam, 1991, pp. 131–199).

Smith, John T. "Medieval Aisled Halls and Their Derivatives" (in *The Archaeological Journal,* Vol. 112, 1955, pp. 76–94).

———. "Medieval Roofs: A Classification" (in *The Archaeological Journal,* Vol. 115, 1958, pp. 111–149).

———. "Timber-Framed Building in England" (in *The Archaeological Journal,* Vol. 122, 1965, pp. 133–158).

———. "The Early Development of Timber Buildings: The Passing-brace and Reversed Assembly" (in *The Archaeological Journal,* Vol. 131, 1974, pp. 238–263).

———. "Romano-British Aisled Houses" (in *The Archeological Journal,* Vol. 120, 1963, pp. 1–28).

———. *The (Cheddar) Buildings. Introduction: Principles of Interpretation and Assumptions Underlying the Reconstructions* (Unpublished manuscript).

———. "The Concept of Diffusion in Its Application to Vernacular Building" (in *Studies in Folk Life,* Routledge & Kegan Paul, 1969, pp. 59–78).

———. *English Houses 1200-1800: The Hertfordshire Evidence* (Royal Commission on the Historical Monuments of England, 1992).

———. "Mittelalterliche Dachkonstruktion in Nordwest-europa" (in *Frühe Holzkirchen im nordlichen Europa,* Claus Ahrens, editor, Hamburg, 1981, pp. 379–390).

———. "The Validity of Inference from Archaeological Evidence" (in *British Archaeological Review,* British Series 110, 1982, pp. 7–19).

———. "Villas, Plans and Social Structure in Britain and Gaul" (in *Caesarodunum,* Universite de Tours, No. 17, 1982, pp. 321–336).

———. "The archaeological investigation of standing buildings" (in *Vernacular Architecture,* No. 20, 1989, p. 20).

Smith, Peter. *Houses of the Welsh Countryside* (2nd edition, London, HMSO, 1988).

Spurr, M. Stephen. *Arable Cultivation in Roman Italy, c. 200 B.C.–c. A.D.* 100 (in *Journal of Roman Studies,* monograph no. 3, London, 1986).

Stadtfeld, Curtis K. *From the Land and Back* (New York, Charles Scribner, 1972).

Stiewe, Heinrich. *Lippische Bauernhöfe des 16.–19. Jahrhunderts* (Schriften des Lippischen Landesmuseums, Vol.1, Ein Beitrag zur Ländlichen Hausforschung, Detmold, 1985).

Stoepker, H. "Church Archaeology in the Netherlands. Problems, Prospects, Proposals" (in *Medieval Archaeology in the Netherlands,* J. C. Besteman, J. M. Bos, and H. A. Heidinga, editors, Maastricht, 1990, pp. 199–218).

Stokes, I. N. Phelps. *The Iconography of Manhattan Island, 1498–1909* (6 vols., New York, R. H. Dodd, 1915–1928).

Stratford, Neil. "Les bâtiments de l'abbaye de Cluny à l'époque médiévale. État des questions" (in *Bulletin Monumental,* Vol. 150, No. 4, Année 1992, pp. 383–411).

Szentendre Open Air Museum. *Regional Units of the Open Air Museum: Upper Tiza Region* (Hungary, Szentendre, 1980).

Talbot, S. J. Francis. *Saint Among Savages: The life of Isaac Jogues* (New York and London, Harper, 1935).

Theophrastus. *Enquiry into Plants* (Trans. A. Hort, Cambridge and London, 1968).

Theuws, F. "Landed Property and Manorial Organisation in Northern Austrasia: Some Considerations and a Case Study" (in *Images of the Past: Studies on Ancient Societies in North-western Europe,* Nico Roymans and Frans Theuws, editors, Instituut voor Pre- en Protohistorische Archeologie Albert Egges van Giffen, Amsterdam, 1991, pp. 299–407).

Theuws, F., A. Verhoeven, and H. H. Van Regteren Altenen. *Medieval Settlement at Dommelen* (Instituut voor Pre- en Protohistorische Archeologie Albert Egges van Giffen, Amsterdam, 1990).

Titow, J. Z. *Winchester Yields: A Study in Medieval Agricultural Productivity* (Cambridge University Press, 1972).

Todd, Malcolm. "Aisled Halls in Roman Gaul" (in *Oxford Journal of Archaeology,* 11[3], 1992, pp. 369–372).

Tosti-Croce, Marina Righetti. *Architettura e economia: "strutture di produzione cistercensi"* (Unidentified source).

Trefois, Clemens V. *Ontwikkelings Geschiedenis van onze Landelijke Architectuur* (Sint Niklaas, 1978).

———. *Van Vakwerk Tot Baksteenbouw* (Sint Niklaas, pp. 87–92).

Trier, Bendix. *Das Haus in Nordwesten der Germania Libera* (Münster, Aschendorff, 1969).

Turner, T. Hudson. *Some Account of Domestic Architecture in England from the Conquest to the End of the Thirteenth Century* (1st edition, Oxford, 1851).

Uilkema, K. *Het Friesche Boerenhuis: onderzoek naar het onstaan van het tegenwoordige boerenhuis in Friesland* (Leeuwarden, 1916).

van Olst, Ellen L. *Uilkema, een historisch boerderij-onderzoek: Boerderij-onderzoek in Nederland, 1914–1934* (Deel I and II, Arnhem, SHBO, 1991).

Verdier, Aymar, and F. Cattois. *Architecture Civile et Domestique au moyen âge et à la renaissance* (2 vols., Paris, 1855/1857).

Viollet-le-Duc, Eugène-Emmanuel. *Dictionnaire raisonné de l'architecture française du XIᵉ au XVIᵉ siècle* (10 vols., Paris, 1854–1868). (The full English translation, made by Nathan Ricker [circa 1917], is available at the Ricker Library, Dept. of Art and Architecture, 608 East Lorado Taft, Champaign, Illinois 61820).

———. *The Architectural Theory of Viollet-le-Duc: Readings and Commentary* (M. F. Hearn, editor, MIT Press, 1992).

———. *The Foundations of Architecture: Selections from the Dictionnaire raisonné* (Trans. K. D. Whitehead, New York, 1990).

Vitruvius. *The Ten Books on Architecture* (Trans. Morris Hicky Morgan, Harvard University Press, 1914).

Wacker, Peter O. *The Musconetcong Valley of New Jersey: A Historical Geography* (Rutgers University Press, 1968).

———. "Traditional House and Barn Types in New Jersey: Keys to Acculturation, Past Cultureographic Regions, and Settlement History" (in *Geoscience and Man,* Vol. 5, *Man and Cultural Heritage,* Louisiana State University, Baton Rouge, 1974, pp. 163–176).

———. *Dutch Barns and Barracks in New Jersey During the Eighteenth Century* (Undated paper).

156

Wade, Jane (editor). *Traditional Kent Buildings* (Nos. 1–6, 1980–1988).

Warren, John. "Greater and Lesser Gothic Roofs: A Study of the Crown-post Roof and Its Antecedents" (in *Vernacular Architecture*, No. 23, 1992, pp. 1–9).

Waterbolk, Harm Tjalling. "Das Mittelalterliche siedlungswesen in Drenthe: versuch einer synthese aus archäologischer sicht" (in *Siedlungen und Landesausbau zur Salierzeit, Teil 1, in den nördlichen landschaften des reiches*, Römisch-Germanisches Zentralmuseum, Monographien, Vol. 27, 1991, pp. 47–108).

————— "Elp" (in *Reallexikon der Germanischen Altertumskunde*, Vol. 7, Lieferung 1/2, 1986, pp. 163–175).

————. "Mobilität von Dorf, Ackerflur und Gräberfeld in Drenthe seit der Latènezeit" (in *Offa: Berichte und Mitteilungen zur Urgeschichte, Frühgeschichte und Mittelalterarchäologie*, Vol. 39, 1982, pp. 97–138. Neumünster, Carl Wacholtz Verlag, 1982).

Webster, Leslie, and Janet Backhouse (editors). *The Making of England: Anglo-Saxon Art and Culture A.D. 600–900* (British Museum Press, 1991).

Weller, John. *Grangia et Orreum—The Medieval Barn: A Nomenclature* (Bildeston, 1986).

————. *Canons' Barn: Wells: Somerset* (Bildeston, 1989).

Weller, J. B., and C. J. Bond. "The Somerset Barns of Glastonbury Abbey" (in *The Archaeology and History of Glastonbury Abbey*, 1991, pp. 57–88).

Weyns, Jozef. *Het Kempisch Boerenhuis* (Belgium, undated).

White, K. D. *Roman Farming* (Ithaca, New York, Cornell University Press, 1970).

————. *Farm Equipment of the Roman World* (Cambridge University Press, 1975).

Widrig, Walter M. *Ancient Roman Villa Gardens: Land Use at the Via Gabina Villas* (Dumbarton Oaks Research Library and Collection, 1987).

————. *Excavations on the Ancient Via Gabina. Second Preliminary Report* (in Atti della Accademia Nazionale Dei Lincei, Anno CCCLXXX, Notizie Degli Scavi Di Antichità, Serie Ottava—Vol. XXXVII, Roma, 1986, pp. 141–182).

Wightman, Edith Mary. *Gallia Belgica* (London, Batsford, 1985).

Wiswe, Hans. "Grangien niedersächsischer Zisterzienserklöster: Entstehung und Bewirtschaftlung spätmittelalterlich-frühneuzeitlicher landwirtschaftlicher Großbetriebe" (in *Braunschweigisches Jahrbuch*, Vol. 34, 1953, pp. 5–134).

Zimmermann, W. Haio. "Economy of the Roman Iron Age Settlement at Flögeln, Kr. Cuxhaven, Lower Saxony. Husbandry, Cattle Farming and Manufacturing" (in *Lowland Iron Age Communities in Europe*, British Archaeological Review, International Series [Supplementary] 48, 1978, pp. 147–165).

—————. "5000 Jahre Siedlung und Wirtschaft im Geestgebiet" (in *Archäologie in Deutschland*, Vol. 1, 1991, pp. 18–23).

—————. *Siedlungsarchäologische Untersuchungen auf der Geest* (Forschung in Wilmhelmshaven).

—————. "Die früh- bis hochmittelalterliche wüstung Dalem gem. langenneuenwalde, Kr. Cuxhaven. Archäologische untersuchungen in einem dorf des 7.–14. jahrhunderts" (in *Siedlungen und Landesausbau zur Salierzeit, Teil 1, in den nördlichen landschaften des reiches*, Römisch-Germanisches Zentralmuseum, Monographien, Vol. 27, 1991, pp. 37–46).

—————. "Die früh- bis hochmittelalterliche Dorfwüstung Dalem, Kr. Cuxhaven" (in *Westvlaamse Archaeologica Monografieën 11*, Kortrijk, 1981, pp. 239–247).

—————. *Probleme der Küstenforschung im Südlichen Nordseegebiet. Vol. 19. Die Siedlungen des 1. bis 6. Jahrhunderts nach Christus von Flögeln-Eekhöltjen, Niedersachsen: Die Bauformen und ihre Funktionen* (Hildesheim, 1992).

—————. "The 'Helm' in England, Wales, Scandinavia and North America" (in *Vernacular Architecture*, No. 23, 1992, pp. 34–43).

Zippelius, Adelhart. "Das Bauernhaus am unteren deutschen niederrhein" (in *Werken und Wohnen: volkskundliche untersuchungen im Rheinland*, Vol. 1, Landschaftsverband Rheinland, Wuppertal, 1957).

—————. "Das vormittelalterliche dreischiffige Hallenhaus in Mitteleuropa" (in *Bonner Jahrbucher des Rheinischen Landesmuseums in Bonn*, Vol. 153, 1953, pp. 13–45).

PICTURE CREDITS

Prologue, 1.3, 1.14, 2.2, 3.3, 3.4, 3.8, 3.9, 3.10, 3.11, 4.11, 4.12, 7.3 Resource Collections of the Getty Center for the History of Art and the Humanities, Santa Monica, California (Walter Horn/Ernest Born Archives No. 920089).

1.17 Resource Collections of the Getty Center for the History of Art and the Humanities, Santa Monica, California (T. Hudson Turner, *Some Account of Domestic Architecture in England from the Conquest to the End of the Thirteenth Century,* Oxford, 1851, frontispiece).

3.1, 7.5 Resource Collections of the Getty Center for the History of Art and the Humanities, Santa Monica, California (Aymar Verdier and F. Cattois, *Architecture Civile et Domestique au moyen âge et à la renaissance,* Paris, 1855/1857).

Color plates 2, 3, 5 The British Library, London (*Luttrell Psalter,* Add. MS. 42130, ff.172ᵛ, 173ᵛ, and 74ᵛ).

Color plate 4 Bayerische Staatsbibliothek, Munich (Clm 28345, fol. 6ᴿ).

2.3 Courtesy of Hans Henrik Engqvist, Lyngby, Denmark.

2.6 Bildarchiv Foto Marburg, Philipps-Universität, Marburg, Germany (Grange d'Ardenne No. 160.003).

4.2 Musée du Bardo, Tunisia.

4.3 Deutsches Archäologisches Institut, Rome.

4.4 After Claus Ahrens, *Frühe Holzkirchen im Nördlichen Europa* (Hamburgisches Museum für Vor- und Frühgeschichte, 1981). See also Adolph Goldschmidt, *Die Eiffenbeinskulpturen* (Berlin, 1914, Vol. 1, p. xxxv, plate 84).

4.5 Landschaftsverband Rheinland, Bonn (*Jungfrauenspiegel* by Konrad Hirsau, No. 15328).

4.6 The Bodleian Library, Oxford (MS. Bodl. 270b, fol. 28ᴿ, roundel bl.).

4.13 Courtesy of Walter Widrig, Rice University, Houston, Texas.

5.7 Westfälisches Baupflegeamt, Münster (drawings by Josef Schepers from *Haus und Hof westfälischer Bauern,* Aschendorff, Münster, 1977).

5.15 RUG Biologisch-Archaeologisch Instituut, Groningen (photograph of Ezinge by A. E. van Giffen, No. E-62871-2).

6.1 (*Top left*), 6.3 Drawings by Jack Sobon.

6.1 (*Bottom right*) Drawing by Michael Boulay.

6.12 Resource Collections of the Getty Center for the History of Art and the Humanities, Santa Monica, California (John Fitchen Archive No. 910018).

6.13 Courtesy of Herman Hagens.

7.2 Collection of the Alte Pinakothek, Munich (Cornelis van Dalem, *Landschaft mit Gehöft,* No. 12044).

7.6 Courtesy of Konrad Bedal (*Fachwerk vor 1600 in Franken: Eine Bestandsaufnahme,* Fränkisches Freilandmuseum, Bad Windsheim, 1990).

8.14 (*Top left*), 8.21 (*top left*) Drawings by Jack Sobon (after H. Janse).

8.14 (*Bottom right*), 8.17, 8.19, 8.21 (*bottom right*) Courtesy of the Stichting Historisch Boederij-onderzoek, Arnhem (redrawn by Jack Sobon).

INDEX

Page numbers in italics indicate black-and-white photographs. Color plates follow page 48.